Creativity and Learning in Secondary English

Creativity in secondary English lessons today is a democratically conceived quality that all pupils are expected to achieve and a resource on which all are entitled to draw. But what exactly is creativity and how does it relate to English? *Creativity and Learning in Secondary English* answers these questions, and others, by arguing for a version of creativity that sees it as an ordinary, everyday part of successful classroom practice, central to processes of meaning-making, dialogic interaction and textual engagement. In this construction, creativity is not just linked to learning; it is the driving force behind learning itself, offering pupils the opportunity to transform their knowledge and understanding of the world around them.

The book borrows from a range of theories about creativity and learning while remaining largely practical in focus. It contains numerous examples for teachers of how to apply ideas about creativity in the classroom. In doing so, it attempts to maintain the subject's core identity while also keeping abreast of contemporary social, pedagogical and technological developments. The result is a refreshing challenge to some of the more mundane approaches to English teaching on offer in an age focused excessively on standardisation and teaching to tests.

Practical applications of creativity include:

- using picturebooks and graphic novels to stimulate multimodal responses;
- placing pupils in the role of the teacher;
- devising marketing campaigns for class novels;
- adopting experimental approaches to redrafting;
- encouraging 'extreme' forms of re-creative writing;
- focusing on how to 'listen' to texts;
- creating sound-scapes for poems.

Thought-provoking and provocative, this textbook draws on current best practice in English teaching and will equip trainee and practising teachers with a wide range of strategies that will lead to greater creativity in the classroom.

Andrew McCallum is Senior Lecturer in Education and Course Leader for Secondary English with Media and Drama at London Metropolitan University.

Creativity and Learning in Secondary English

Teaching for a creative classroom

Andrew McCallum

Routledge
Taylor & Francis Group

LONDON AND NEW YORK

First published 2012
by Routledge
2 Park Square, Milton Park, Abingdon, Oxon OX14 4RN

Simultaneously published in the USA and Canada
by Routledge
711 Third Avenue, New York, NY 10017

Routledge is an imprint of the Taylor & Francis Group, an informa business

British Library Cataloguing in Publication Data
A catalogue record for this book is available from the British Library

Library of Congress Cataloging-in-Publication Data
McCallum, Andrew.
Creativity and learning in secondary English : teaching for a creative
classroom / Andrew McCallum.
  p. cm.
1. English language--Composition and exercises--Study and teaching
(Secondary) 2. Creative ability. I. Title.
LB1631.M3937 2012
808'.0420712--dc23
2011042465

ISBN: 978-0-415-62069-7 (hbk)
ISBN: 978-0-415-62070-3 (pbk)
ISBN: 978-0-203-12248-8 (ebk)

Typeset in Bembo
by Keystroke, Station Road, Codsall, Wolverhampton

Printed and bound in Great Britain by
TJ International Ltd, Padstow, Cornwall

To Anna

Contents

List of illustrations   *xi*
Acknowledgements   *xiii*
Image credits   *xv*

Introduction   1
A summary of content   2

Part I The role of creativity in English   7

1 English and creativity: A brief history   9
   Beginnings: rationing creativity   10
   Continuation: creativity helps you grow   11
   Re-orientation: the creativity of everyday life   13
   Rupture: deconstructing creativity   14
   Re-construction 1: from critical literacy to a new aesthetic   15
   Re-construction 2: creativity and genre   16
   Re-construction 3: multimodality   17
   Conclusion   18
   Key texts   19

2 Theories of creativity, English and learning   20
   Evolutionary creativity   21
   Linguistic creativity   23
   Literary creativity   27
   Ordinary creativity and making meaning   30
   Conclusion   32
   Key texts   33

Part II Creativity and the English curriculum   35

3 Creativity, English and modality   37
   Re-positioning the verbal   38
   Images and words   41

Reading images 42
Combining words and still images in children's picturebooks 46
Exploring the mode of sound 50
Conclusion 52
Key texts 53

4 Creativity as re-creativity   54
Developing a theory of re-creativity 56
From re-telling to re-writing 58
Writer-response: an alternative form of reading 62
Re-creativity and possible worlds 63
Extreme re-creativity 67
Conclusion 72
Key texts 73

5 Creativity and the class novel   74
What is the creativity of the novel and why is it important to English? 75
Extending the vocabulary of creativity 77
Vocabulary point no. 1: textualness/authoredness 78
Vocabulary point no. 2: ethics/otherness 80
Vocabulary point no. 3: text as event 82
Creativity, class-readers and choice 83
Conclusion 87
Key texts 87

6 Listening, reading and creativity   88
Reading with the ear 90
Listening to how others read 94
Critical listening: voice and the class reader 95
Conclusion 101
Key texts 101

7 Speaking, writing and creativity   102
Links between speaking and writing 103
Differences between speaking and writing 105
Conclusion 108
Key texts 110

8 Critical-creativity   111
A critique of critique 112
Bringing creativity and criticality together 113
Paulo Freire: critical literacy, creativity and praxis *113*
Key concepts in Freire's idea of praxis *114*
P.E.E.: limiting criticality and creativity 115
Critical-creativity and wholeness 117

Newspaper work: from a skills-based to a critical-creative approach   118
Students as teachers: critical-creativity and role-play   122
Re-drafting as a critical-creative process   123
Conclusion   127
Key texts   128

9 Creativity and culture   129
The creativity of a common culture   130
From a common culture to multiculturalism   132
Multiculturalism and idioculture   133
What has all this to do with English and creativity?   133
Transforming cultures   134
Using Manga Shakespeare   134
The creativity of emerging cultures: gaming lessons for the non-gaming teacher   139
Traditional text as hypertext   142
Conclusion   144
Key texts   145

Conclusion: Creativity and *not* learning   146
Assessment for not learning   147
Not learning *objectives*   147
Not *a plenary*   148
Not *literature*   148
Not *a text type*   148
Not *correctness*   148
Not *describing*   149
Not *vocabulary*   149
Not *writing*   149
Not *reading*   150

References   *151*
Index   *157*

Illustrations

Figures

3.1   Image from Shaun Tan's *The Arrival* (2007)   42
3.2   Image from Eileen Browne's *Handa's Surprise* (1994)   47
3.3   Image from Anthony Browne's *Hansel and Gretel* (1981)   48
8.1   'Attacking from rear', *Daily Mirror*, 12 January 2011   119
8.2   'Model soldier ready for war', *Daily Mirror*, 12 January 2011   121
9.1   Cover of Oscar Grillo's illustrated version of *The Tempest* (2009)   136
9.2   Page from Robert Deas's *Manga Shakespeare: Macbeth* (2008)   137
9.3   Cover of Hugo Petrus and Nancy Butler's illustrated version of
      Pride and Prejudice (2010)   140

Boxes

1.1   The changing nature of creativity   18
3.1   Contemporary images with traditional narratives   48
3.2   The transition from still to moving images   49
3.3   Giving meaning to nonsense   49
3.4   Sound first: Building up to the creativity of the whole   50
4.1   Re-telling creatively   59
4.2   Telling the story of a book cover   60
4.3   Multiple ways to *transform* a text   64
4.4   Writing modern-day fairy stories   65
4.5   Transforming fiction   65
4.6   Playing with genre   66
4.7   Multiple writings   68
4.8   Re-creating poems   70
4.9   Extremely extreme re-creativity   71
5.1   Hot-seating the author   79
5.2   Marketing a novel   79
5.3   Holding a novel to trial   81
5.4   How does a novel make you *feel*?   81

5.5	Video journals	82
5.6	Instant re-creation	83
5.7	Tableaux	83
5.8	Voting on which novel to read next	85
6.1	Reading for sense before meaning	91
6.2	Asking questions about a text	91
6.3	Sound tunnels	92
6.4	Poem as sound	93
6.5	Sound modelling	93
6.6	Listening to the author's voice	94
6.7	Reading the 'voices' in an extract	96
6.8	Reproducing dialogue	97
6.9	Exploring a range of voices	98
6.10	Unheard voices	99
6.11	Performing sounds	99
7.1	Analysing the creativity of *speech-as-writing*	104
7.2	Story-telling in the round	106
7.3	Verbal tennis	106
7.4	Speaking to a writing frame	106
7.5	Speaking-to-writing-to-speaking-to-writing	107
7.6	Dismantling a text	108
8.1	Using models for redrafts	124
8.2	Studying how others redraft	125
8.3	Redrafting according to set instructions	126
9.1	From text to hypertext	143

Acknowledgements

The idea for this book sprang from an informal meeting with Annamarie Kino at Routledge. I am extremely grateful for her initial encouragement and continued advice and support. It is fair to say that without that meeting the book would not have come into being. I would also like to thank Hamish Baxter for his assured editorial guidance.

The irony of writing this book about English teaching is that it would not have come about if I had remained in the classroom. Working for three years as a PGCE tutor at London Metropolitan University has allowed me to reflect on fifteen years spent previously in London secondary schools. I am extremely grateful for this opportunity and would like to thank my fellow PGCE tutors, Alan Benson, Marcus Bhargava, Victoria Brook, Suzanne Burley, David Cross, Greg Dryer and Rebecca Smith, for their stimulating conversation and ideas. Special mention should go to Lee Jerome, a fabulous team leader, who has always encouraged me to present conference papers and pursue my research interests. I would also like to thank the hundred or so trainees who have taken the PGCE in English with Media and Drama during my time at the university. I have learned something from each and every one, especially about the benefits of collaborative learning. Particular mention should go to several individuals from whom I have drawn ideas: Anna Bowen, Jessica Browning, Apala Choudhury, Bob Glanville and Lucy Lawrence. I'd also like to single out Arnaud Mugglestone (along with his colleague Bo Fowler) for his help and enthusiasm in the early stages of this project. The ideas about encouraging pupils to teach lessons all stem from work Arnaud carried out while completing his PGCE.

I owe a debt of gratitude to another institution: Acland Burghley School, in Camden. Site of my first teaching post and the base for most of my career, it has a progressive spirit and tradition that stands as a beacon of hope in the face of some of the more dominant, conformist strains in current educational thinking. I learned from many of my colleagues while working there and would like to give particular thanks to everyone I worked with in the English department.

Before I began writing I knew very little about picturebooks. The fact that they occupy considerable space in what follows is down to my good fortune in teaming up with Pam Dix to teach a Masters module in Children's Literature. Pam introduced me to most of the picturebooks mentioned in the pages that follow and the idea about how to use *Handa's Surprise* I borrowed from her in its entirety. I hope those who read this book will be inspired to take picturebooks into the secondary classroom, as I have been by Pam.

I would like to thank several colleagues with whom I have worked over the past few years for their general advice. While they have not necessarily contributed directly to the contents of the book, they have all influenced and impressed me with their commitment to making sure English remains a vibrant subject. In particular, I would like to thank Ammar Al-Gabban, Alison Feist, Maggi Fisher, Philippa Hunt, Laura Sparkes, John Wilks, and Marilyn Wright. Intellectual stimulation has been equally forthcoming from my friends, Stephen Donovan and Mark Flynn.

I would also like to mention the Woodlands Park gang for allowing me to get my work done by relieving me of childcare duties on many occasions. Thank you Vanessa Cooke, Jerzy Gromiski, Jess MacGregor, Damien Parrott, Sam Raphael and Bethan Williams. Also thanks to my parents Malcolm and Kate McCallum and my (many) in-laws, Martin Bridge, Annie McCabe, Steve Rimington and especially Pip Bridge. In a similar vein I would like to thank Gloria Rego and her care team for looking after my eldest son, Joe, with such dedication and kindness.

Finally, and most importantly, I'd like to thank my family, my three sons, Joe, Nate and Fran for making life so much fun, and Anna for being the most wonderful partner anyone could wish for. There's no way I could have written the book without you.

Image credits

Every effort has been made to trace copyright holders, but in some instances this has not been possible. The publishers would like to apologise for any errors or omissions, and would appreciate being advised of any corrections that should be made to future editions of the book.

Pride and Prejudice illustrated version, by Hugo Petrus and Nancy Butler © Marvel Entertainment and used with permission.

'The Arrival' image reproduced with permission from *The Arrival* by Shaun Tan, Lothian Children's Books, an imprint of Hachette Australia, 2006.

Illustration from *Hansel and Gretel* by Anthony Browne © 1981, 2003 Anthony Browne, reproduced by permission of Walker Books Ltd, London SE11 5HJ.

Illustration from *Handa's Surprise* by Eileen Browne © 1994 Eileen Browne, reproduced by permission of Walker Books Ltd, London SE11 5HJ.

'Attacking From Rear: MoD tells girls: boozing makes you fat', by Chris Hughes, and 'Model Soldier Ready for War', by Krissy Storrar, reproduced with permission from the *Daily Mirror*.

Manga Shakespeare: Macbeth, by Robert Deas and Richard Appignanesi (2008), reproduced with permission from SelfMadeHero.

Introduction

> . . . creativity and self-creation are both known and unknown events, and it is still from grasping the known that the unknown – the next step, the next work – is conceived.
>
> Raymond Williams, *Marxism and Literature*

I'd like to start with two contrasting questions. The first is a brainteaser: *How can ten students create one hundred thousand billion poems in an hour?* The second is more obvious: *What is creativity?* A straightforward answer to the first is provided at the end of the introduction. A definitive response to the second is far more complicated and I make no pretences to having one. For creativity has many meanings and many uses. It can as readily apply to acts of individual genius (Scruton 2000) as it can to collective forms of cultural participation (Willis 1990); it is equally applicable to extraordinary feats in science and the arts (Gardner 1993) as it is to the everyday functions of language (Carter 2004); and it is at one and the same time a tool for social good, producing outcomes that are "of value" (NACCCE 1999), and a necessity for economic success (Leadbetter 2000). Its extensive use is demonstrated in a literature review that identifies nine broad "rhetorics of creativity" (Banaji and Burn 2008), including "democratic and political creativity", "creativity as social good" and "the creative affordances of technology".

In education creativity can refer simultaneously to a style of teachers, to what is taught and to how learning occurs (NACCCE 1999; Jeffrey and Craft 2003). In recent years it has been the focus of several policy documents (NACCCE 1999; QCA 2005; Safford and Barrs 2005; Roberts 2006; Ofsted 2010) and academic books (Craft, Jeffrey and Leibling 2001; Beghetto and Kaufman 2010; Starko 2010), which stress its importance to successful learning.

All this begs the question, why yet another book on creativity? The answer lies in the particular relationship between secondary school English and creativity promoted in these pages. For while a great deal of attention has been paid to exploring the process of creativity as it relates to learning across the curriculum, this generally involves investigating how young people learn through *being creative*. This is absolutely a key focus for learning in English (Grainger, Gooch and Lambirth 2005; Cremin 2009) and is addressed in these pages. However, little corresponding attention has been paid to the creativity that available resources bring *to* learning.

This is particularly pertinent to English given the creativity inherent in language, literature and other forms of communication and representation. Thus this book has two main concerns: how young people learn through being creative in English, and how the creativity of English helps young people learn.

The book tries to take a contemporary approach to English without losing sight of the creativity offered by its traditional staples, language and literature. It is indebted to several key works in treading this path between what has gone before and what the future promises. Ronald Carter's (2004) idea of 'ordinary creativity' helps distance the book fully from the now discredited belief that linguistic creativity only resides in great works of literature. Gunther Kress's extensive work (1982, 1993, 1995, 2000, 2003, 2010; Kress *et al.* 2005) on English and related fields such as genre and multi-modality is invaluable in providing ideas as to how the subject might transform itself in order to adapt to the modern world. Some of his ideas, however, are also challenged, not so much for their usefulness to learning, as for the degree to which they push aside other aspects of the subject. For the book is also keen to preserve a central role for literature, drawing on innovative work by Richard Kearney (1988, 2002), Derek Attridge (2004) and Rob Pope (2005) in the field of English Studies and linking it to attempts to reclaim the role of 'the aesthetic' in the classroom (Misson and Morgan 2006, 2007). Each of these authors at some point draws on at least one of three Russian theorists, Lev Vygotsky (1986 [1936]), Valentin Volosinov (2000) and Mikhail Bakhtin (2006). Their groundbreaking ideas about the dialogic function of language and thought are referenced liberally throughout this book.

A summary of content

Creativity and Learning in Secondary English is split into two sections. The first gives an overview of the relationship between English and creativity as a foundation for the more practical chapters that follow. Chapter 1 gives a historical account of the relationship between English and creativity. It attempts to understand what creativity means to the subject now by thinking closely about what it meant in the past. It identifies how applications of creativity have shifted broadly in line with developments in the subject itself and describes its radical repositioning over the past half-century or so: from a position where it was conceived of as lying in the hands of a few creative artists to one where it describes the ordinary, everyday activity by which the many can generate new meaning through various communicative acts. This fundamental shift is given theoretical grounding in Chapter 2, which looks at creativity as it pertains to key aspects of English: to language, to literature and to symbolic forms of representation in general. Wider debates about the meaning of creativity and its links to learning in other fields are touched upon but only as they relate to the particular form and significance creativity has to English. This is in keeping with a focus on the centrality of language to both creativity and learning. The focus is not intended to exclude other modes of meaning-making but to question the levels and types of learning they encourage compared to an engagement with the spoken and written word.

The seven chapters in the second section each explore the relationship of creativity to a different aspect of English teaching and learning. The decision to lead with a chapter on creativity and modality reflects the desire to situate contemporary notions of how the subject might be transformed within the bounds of current practice. Thus multimodality is presented as having a key role to play in the subject's future, while particular attention is given to the familiar verbal modes of speaking and writing. This blending of the current and the traditional is continued in Chapter 4, which looks at *re*-creativity. Re-creativity encourages students actively to give new form and meaning to texts and to reflect on the transformations they bring about. It offers a blend of the creative and the critical in encouraging learners to make something afresh but also to reflect on what any transformations suggest about an original.

Chapter 5 explores the creativity of the class reader. It argues for the continuing importance of novels in English, with a focus on their *transactional* qualities as they both *act on* readers and are *acted upon*. It draws in particular on the work of Attridge (2004), and Misson and Morgan (2006, 2007) to demonstrate how ideas about 'the singularity of literature' and 'the aesthetic' can be reclaimed for the subject. Thus the creativity texts bring to readers – what texts *do* to readers – is given importance alongside the creativity that readers bring to texts.

Chapters 6 and 7 re-order the 'profile components' of English, so that *speaking and listening* and *reading and writing* become *listening and reading* and *speaking and writing* (Alexander 2008). Chapter 6 conceives of listening and reading as analogous to one another. It sees both as having a key role to play in understanding the creativity *in* texts in order to place creativity *on* texts. This involves students being engaged in both *active reading* and *active listening*. In Chapter 7, speaking and writing are seen as complementary rather than analogous. Both are the generative processes by which meaning is brought into being. As such, the chapter explores how one can draw on the other in order to stimulate creativity.

Chapter 8 draws on Paulo Freire's (1996 [1970]) idea of *praxis* as it combines elements of 'action' and 'reflection' to consider how a *critical-creativity* might be conceived of in the classroom. The chapter questions the value of 'critique' to the subject today and looks at how particular creative and re-creative practices offer a way to maintain and rejuvenate its use.

Chapter 9 explores the practical applications of creativity as it links to ideas of *culture*. It takes a broad view of culture as 'a way of life'. This allows learners to draw on all elements of their existence in the classroom, generating meaning as the multiple perspectives on offer come into contact with each other and with new material. It also seeks to offer a broad definition of *multiculturalism* and explores how the particular orientation of this word is important in order to broaden rather than limit opportunities for creativity.

The conclusion is deliberately provocative in its title, 'Creativity and not learning'. It challenges teachers to think carefully about the implications of standardised approaches to teaching and learning and to consider the wider consequences of educational systems that place an excessive value on measuring performance and examination success. The term 'not learning' is not intended to encourage a culture of ignorance, but surmises that if there is 'learning' then there must be '*not* learning', an idea developed by Gunter Kress (2010) in exploring how the parameters within which learning takes place are set by those with institutional power.

So, ironically, it seems a book with learning in its title ultimately seeks to reject learning. Of course, this is not absolutely the case, for most of the learning going on in the English educational system is benign at worst and, despite the rhetoric from government benches, in many ways progressive and inspirational. However, the book does want to warn against excessively standardised teaching approaches where they do occur and, in turn, promote classroom approaches that challenge rather than accept dominant norms, that move towards contestation rather than compliance. Radical and utopian ideals aside, this is in a spirit of *genuine* learning, of enabling young people to take control, to as large a degree as possible, of the circumstances in which they live. They can only have control if they are able to bring shape to their lives. 'Ordinary creativity' is an apt term for describing this process: recognising the transformative nature of the material with which we shape our existence, particularly language, and striving to put it to good effect.

Censure of an approach that values 'ordinary creativity' might claim that it devalues creativity, spreading its application too thinly for it to have any real meaning. But emphasising its ordinary, everyday nature is intended to provoke the opposite response. It draws to attention the astonishing potential that exists in the material we use to make sense of our daily lives. Creativity offers a way of describing the activation of that potential and so of transforming the co-ordinates of our existence – of advancing learning – no matter in how small a way. In classrooms it might occur through adopting very simple strategies, such as structuring talk in lessons so as to generate a range of new ideas and perspectives on source material, or it might come in drawing attention to the astonishing versatility humans possess for symbolic representation, particularly in language. This point leads neatly back to the question at the start about ten students writing a hundred thousand billion poems in an hour. The answer lies in directing each to write a single fourteen-line sonnet. These are then combined to replicate a technique used by Raymond Queneau in writing *100,000,000,000,000 Poems* (Queneau in Mathews and Brotchie 2005). He wrote ten sonnets and arranged them one on top of the other. A serrated line separates each line of poetry which readers must cut along so that the line can be lifted away to reveal another underneath. The mathematics of this process are explained as follows:

> Start with the first line taken in isolation: there are, obviously, 10 alternatives or possibilities for it. When we now add a line, we know that each of the 10 first lines can be followed by any of the 10 second lines: this gives us $10 \times 10 = 100$ (or 10^2) possible combinations of two lines. Each of these combinations of two lines can in turn be followed by any one of the 10 third lines, a step that will produce $10 \times 100 = 1,000$ (or 10^3) possible combinations of *three* lines. In similar fashion, every additional line raises the number of possible combinations by a factor of 10 until, with the 14th line, we attain 10^{14} possible combinations of fourteen lines, a number that can be variously written as 100

billion (UK), 100,000 billion (US), or 10 million million – a very large number however you write it. Queneau calculated that someone reading the book 24 hours a day would need 190,258,751 years to finish it.

(Mathews and Brotchie 2005: 14)

The resulting poems are not especially memorable, nor, in the case of the students combining poems written individually, will they make particular sense. However, as a simple task it demonstrates the astonishing creative capacity of language, one that even extends beyond Queneau's mathematical formulation. For Queneau relies as much on the ability of mathematics to generate a huge number of combinations from a relatively small base as he does on qualities intrinsic to language; but the flexibility of the human mind means that each reading of each poem generates its own particular, additional meaning. This book locates itself within such creativity, so that we might begin to conceive of it not only as ordinary but also as extraordinary; ordinary in that it draws on processes open to us all and extraordinary in that its parameters are almost boundless. 'Almost' is perhaps the key word in this sentence. For if creativity involves the generation of new meaning, and meaning refers to what can be understood, it must presumably push at constraints without breaking free entirely. Meaning, after all, has to mean. It needs to be situated in what is already known. Learning has a similar relationship to constraints. It must recognise them, but in order to progress must look beyond them, never to break free entirely, but never merely to accept and acquiesce. Creativity brings new meaning into being. Learning brings new meaning into being. Creativity is learning. Learning is creativity.

Part I

The role of creativity in English

1

English and creativity
A brief history

Linguistic creativity is not simply a property of exceptional people but an exceptional property of all people.

Ron Carter, *Language and Creativity: The art of common talk*

Creativity is a word much associated with English teachers and English teaching. English practitioners (along with their music colleagues) are, after all, the ones most likely to be portrayed as creative and interested in the creativity of their students in popular representations of school (Harris, Jarvis and Fisher 2008). It is not, however, a word that, until the last decade or so, has necessarily occurred widely in either official documents or academic writing about the subject. Its absence from the first is not particularly surprising. As a term that is difficult to define and that generally alludes to processes equally difficult to quantify, it holds restricted appeal for those setting official curricula and guidance. Its limited presence in academic writing is perhaps more surprising. A history of the subject (Shayer 1972) might well identify a "creativity movement" (40), influential from the 1940s through to the 1970s, but the word still rarely appears in work by those associated with this movement.

There are several possibilities as to why there is a discrepancy between the actual use of creativity and perceptions of its use. First, it is not used as an abstract noun until 1875 (Pope 2005: 1). Prior to that the related terms of 'creator', 'creation' and 'create' are generally applied to acts of supreme beings, with notions of 'creative art' as a human activity only beginning to emerge in the work of the Romantic poets at the beginning of the nineteenth century. It is rarely used to refer to human actions until the 1940s and 1950s. Also, particularly in its early use, a clear distinction is drawn between 'creativity' and 'being creative'. The former applies to the actions of an elite few, those who can offer an image of the world in keeping with its previous connotations of a divine presence, while the latter applies to more humble attempts to replicate this creativity. Additionally, by the 1970s it is often used in a pejorative sense to connote a lack of rigour and formal structure in language-based learning, perhaps resulting in the development of alternative terms within progressive branches of English.

Sketching a brief history of English and creativity, then, can present problems. For it seeks to explore a process not necessarily referred to directly and sometimes actively avoided. Thus it draws on instances where the word creativity is used but also refers to work that might well have used it had it been written at a different time.

Providing an overview of creativity as it has been used and constructed in the past is intended to throw light on how it is used and constructed now, to take us to a moment when, far from being absent from official discourse in England, it is embedded in the latest version of the National Curriculum (QCDA 2007) as one of its four *key concepts*. The method employed – though on a much more modest scale – mirrors that of Kearney (1988) in his exploration of 'the imagination'. He writes that "the term we are seeking to define can only be defined by means of the search itself" (17) and that "we cannot know exactly what imagination *is* until we first narrate the genealogical tales of its becoming, the stories of its genesis". We cannot understand creativity now without understanding what it was in the past.

The brief genealogical tales of English and creativity that follow in some ways make for peculiar reading. For the version of creativity with which we begin is almost diametrically opposed to that with which we end. The word, as if reflecting its use to describe the process by which something comes into being, seems constantly to be coming into being itself, taking on new configurations according to the demands of the subject at a particular time. Traces of its early usage, however, remain today both in the subject's pedagogical approaches and its curriculum content. For any new construction cannot completely avoid the past from which it seeks to move on.

Beginnings: rationing creativity

The first full-length book about English as taught in schools, George Sampson's (1922) *English for the English* sets out to show how it should strive "to give the whole English people a humane, creative education in and through the treasures of their own language and literature" (104). The foundations of the subject, then, have clear links in some way to creativity. However, it is worth noting that the word 'creativity' itself does not occur in Sampson's work. This is not surprising in itself, given that it is rarely applied to human actions for a further twenty years. Closer examination of what he means by "creative education", however, suggests that, were it to have been used, it would have been in a very precise way, one not in keeping with the apparently egalitarian connotations a contemporary reader is likely to derive from a quotation drawing on the words "humane" and "creative".

While Sampson sees creative education as an entitlement for all students, he does not see all students as being – or even having the potential for being – creative. For example, in discussing writing, he expects students to have "the ability to state" (64) but not "the ability to create" although he is "ready to give them credit for genuine attempts at creation". Proficiency "in the use of his native tongue", which Sampson sees as "the universal tool of all callings and of all conditions" is required "before the English child can awaken to any creative fullness of life" (14). Note the use of "any": there is no guarantee that the child will attain this fullness, as Sampson makes clear in warning teachers against thinking that "because everybody uses words in daily speech, creative art in the medium of words is easy or possible to everybody" (62).

"Creative art in the medium words" we might take as referring to literature, what Sampson calls "the English that is not a routine, but a religion" (76). Tellingly it is placed in opposition to "daily speech". For literature at this time, building on ideas established by the Romantic poets and developed by Matthew Arnold (1971 [1869]), is equated almost exclusively with 'creative' and 'imaginative' works (Eagleton 1983: 16) of an exceptional quality that offer spiritual nourishment as a counter-force to the alienating influences of industry and mechanisation. Given this literary source of nourishment is constructed as a replacement for the waning authority of organised religion, it is unsurprising that not everyone is capable of creativity himself or herself. Instead, all may attempt to learn from it even as they cannot partake of it. Thus Sampson argues that "the reading of literature is a kind of creative reception" (76). This is very much a passive form of reception. The reader is literally positioned as the recipient of an author's creativity, rather than as someone bringing meaning to a text in the way he or she receives it. It is also referred to as a process of "re-creation" (78). Again, there is no connotation of active engagement. It simply means that the reading process replicates the creativity of an author in bringing a text (in the same form) into being once more.

To Sampson, then, a "creative education" is one in which creativity is brought to students, primarily in the form of literature. This can help students to be creative themselves, but only in limited ways, for they can never reach the levels of creativity present in the source material itself. Sampson does not draw particularly on phrases common to those writing in a progressive tradition just before him (Macmillan 1904; Holmes 1911; Caldwell Cook 1919; Tudor Owen 1920), phrases such as 'self-expression', 'self-realisation', 'whole being' and 'growth' that become central to a discourse of English as the twentieth century progresses. However, his reference to the "scarcely existent self" (62) of a pupil is indicative of the subject's future orientation towards ideas of helping this 'self' to 'grow' and move towards 'wholeness'. The next section sets out how literature, the embodiment of creativity, becomes the site for exploring progressive educational aims, in particular of *growth* and *self-expression*, the site for *being creative*, if not for achieving full blown *creativity*.

Continuation: creativity helps you grow

While F. R. Leavis provides the dominant influence on English teaching in the decades following Sampson's book, he offers little to advance a model of creativity for teaching. If anything, his work sets creativity at a further remove from everyday life. It positions literature, the embodiment of creativity, not so much as a means to move individuals towards completion, but as protection against the pernicious influences of mass culture, making anxious calls for citizens to "be trained to discriminate and resist" (Leavis and Thompson 1950 [1933]). Much of Leavis's work is directed towards training an elite corps of teachers, able to hand on the benefits of studying literature to the mass of the population (though the masses would never 'get it' to the same degree as the elite). Thus access to creativity becomes staged, teachers providing critical commentary in acting as intermediaries between writers and readers, guardians to the creativity locked within great works.

Those trained directly by Leavis establish the dominant currents in English teaching in what has been called "the post-1945 creativity movement" in English teaching (Shayer 1972: 40). The separation between the creativity of the literary artist and the creative efforts of the child remains in place, though with greater focus on the latter *being* creative. Literature does not so much fill in gaps as show the way for students to unlock the creative energies lying dormant in them. 'Growth' becomes the dominant metaphor in this model, with literature guiding people *towards* a state of completion. The first significant example is Marjorie Hourd's (1949) *The Education of the Poetic Spirit*, which develops a theory of "growth through literature" (14) in which she argues that students need exposure to the likes of Shakespeare, Keats and Coleridge in order to develop an appropriate creativity; as she explains, the child "may read trash when he is alone, but when he becomes creative, in the presence of creators, only the highest standards are appropriate to his efforts" (14). Hourd advances the concept of creativity as it relates to English teaching in that she sees the products of students as genuinely creative, subjecting their work to critical analysis in the same way as she would a Shakespearean sonnet. In this she belongs to a tradition in art education (Viola 1942; Read 1943) that sees young people as being able to create genuine works of art, if not in terms of form and content, then at least in terms of expression. David Holbrook's work draws on similar ideas, most notably *English for Maturity* (1961), which seizes the opportunity offered by the introduction of secondary modern schools to "invent [one's] own methods of work, and start again from scratch" (8). Such methods lead to creativity being constructed as a pedagogical approach as well as a quality of expression, so that it becomes linked to issues of access and democratic entitlement. Students can escape the mental confinement of a functional social and educational system by learning through literature how to open up to their own inner creativity and, consequently, move towards a state of completion. The teacher, however, is very much in control of how this creativity is accessed and what counts as creativity. To Holbrook, starting from scratch means that the English teacher is free "[to] spend all his time, if he wishes, reading with the children just the novels, stories and poetry which he likes himself" (8). The influence of Leavis is clear here: the teacher is the trained expert able to recognise the creativity in literature; through opening the eyes of young people to that creativity, he or she helps them to grow by producing their own creative work. The greater the 'deficit' in the child, the greater the potential of a creative approach to help, asserted Holbrook (1964), in *English for the Rejected*, arguing that "nourishing what I call the poetic function is certainly the most important work with less able children" (10). This is part of a belief that such children can only understand the external world in which they live if they understand more fully the internal world they inhabit. Consequently "a teacher of backward children" should give most importance to the "free, informal, imaginative and often pleasurable and rewarding work of creative English". Holbrook's lack of concern for the formal structures of schools and the curriculum is indicative of a growing link between creativity and alternative approaches to education, giving a radical edge to Sampson's (1922) much earlier claim that English is "not a school subject at all" but "a condition of school life" (24). The implication is that other subjects direct students towards the conformity and sterility of life in an industrial society; English offers a way of maintaining contact with an inner creativity in opposition to this society, through which its true nature can be laid bare.

Re-orientation: the creativity of everyday life

In 1966 more than fifty influential English practitioners from around the globe met for a month-long seminar in Dartmouth, New Hampshire. A significant shift in attitudes to the subject and to creativity is evident in the contrast between two resulting publications. In one, Holbrook (1968) continues to develop his theory of creativity. It adds little to his previous work, and has passed into obscurity. The other, John Dixon's (1967) report on conference proceedings, *Growth through English*, stands as one of the most influential books about the subject of the past half-century. While the inclusion of the word 'growth' in the title provides a link to previous ideas, it marks a shift away from literature to a new focus on "culture as the pupil knows it" (3). Creativity no longer stems from drawing on inner resources to offer a representation of 'external reality', but through working with the material of that 'external reality' to give it shape and meaning relevant to one's own life. Growth, then, no longer applies to a deficit model, whereby the teacher's role is to provide for what is lacking in a young person's character, but to a process of building on what is already there, adding to, developing and extending.

Towards the end of his report Dixon hints that it does not go far enough and that soon "a new model will be needed . . . to redirect our attention to life as it really is" (114). This model takes shape in the additional chapter of a later edition (Dixon 1975), which argues that the initial report pays insufficient attention to language. It also makes a distinction between "expressive" and "communicative" language (136). The former is concerned with "the act of representing" (128) and the latter with bringing clarity to writing that might, for example, report, explain or advise. Expression is privileged over communication because it enables students to place their own ideas on the world. In written work, this means that importance is given to the *process* of writing, rather than to ideas about correctness. Students draw on their own resources for initial drafts before working alongside teachers to make modifications and clarifications in redrafting. It also means that a new importance is given to using talk in the classroom, as explored fully in influential work of the time that includes Barnes, Britton and Rosen's *Language, the Learner and the School* (1969), Britton's *Language and Learning* (1993 [1970]) and Barnes's

From Communication to Curriculum (1976). Talk offers an unmediated and immediate route to self-expression. Additionally it points towards a version of creativity that comes through dialogue, identifying talk as "a means of modifying each other's representations of experience" so that "much of what we build is built in common" (Britton 1993 [1970]: 19). This is creativity manifested as a proliferation of meaning constructed in social interaction.

Notably the word 'creativity' itself rarely occurs in any of the works referred to above, whether exploring speaking or writing. This is interesting to a contemporary reader, given that creativity is now often linked to accessing material through talk (Grainger, Gooch and Lambirth 2005) and to a *process*-model of writing (Robinson and Ellis 2000; Grainger, Gooch and Lambirth 2005). Perhaps its absence at the time marks a conscious attempt to move away from previous connotations of creativity. It might also be an attempt to avoid association with the increasingly pejorative use of the term in relation to education. *A Language for Life* (Bullock 1975), an influential government report on English teaching that places emphasis on language learning, refers to a perception of "unchecked creativity" (6) in schools resulting from a shift from "formal" to "permissive" methods of teaching, though it does not find such a shift to be the case in actual practice.

Rupture: deconstructing creativity

Historical overviews of English written in the 1980s (Baldick 1983; Eagleton 1983; Hunter 1988) call into question the very nature of the subject. Their deconstructive approaches position it not as a means to self-expression and personal growth but as a way of pacifying and controlling the general population. Thus Eagleton's (1983) Marxist critique argues that it is "part of the ideological apparatus of the state" (174), with teachers "custodians of discourse" (175) whose "task is to preserve this discourse, extend and elaborate on it as necessary", while Hunter's (1988) Foucauldian analysis sees it being developed at the start of the twentieth century as part of "a new machinery of government aimed at the 'moral and physical' well-being of whole populations" (ix). Hunter is particularly damning of the links drawn between literature and ideas of self-expression and personal growth, arguing that this involves "the contraction of the morally managed space of the school into the landscape of the literary text" (67). In other words, self-expression is not about students using language creatively in pursuit of their own essential selves, but about them being co-opted to move towards a notion of completeness exemplified – though never fully delineated – in the creative force of literature.

Hunter gives considerable space in his book to attacking Dixon's ideas in *Growth through English*. To a large extent this is based on an early paragraph about students reading literature in the light of their own "personal culture" (Dixon 1967: 3). Hunter points out that when Dixon calls for teachers "to help bring the two into a fruitful relationship" (3), this does not assist young people in self-expression, but leads them into modifying or even correcting their behaviour (1988: 124). The attack is misplaced on three accounts. First, it does not consider the constraints under which Dixon writes. Compiling a report on such a large conference requires sensitivity to a wide range of interests, many of which would express particular ideas about literature that Dixon could not brush aside entirely. As explained above, he does hint at the need to look beyond the model his report offers. Second, Hunter does not consider Dixon's additional chapter in a subsequent edition and the paradigm shift it marks from a focus on literature to one on language. Finally it fails to recognise the meaning that young readers can place *on* literature. Dixon's book makes no mention of a moral imperative whereby readers are *shaped* by literature; rather it shows an awareness of the dialogic processes at work at the meeting point between reader and text.

In a sense Dixon's work recognises the inadequacies of early models of English in much the same way as Eagleton and Hunter, only it is not articulated as criticism, but rather looks for re-orientations in approach that give far greater agency to students, focusing on how they can construct a sense of self through drawing on the available resources in the world at large (including literature) rather than on how they need to rely exclusively on literature to make good a deficit in their being. Subsequent work on the history of English (Dixon 1991; Rose 2002) from the perspective of its use by working-class groups striving for self-improvement in the late nineteenth century, demonstrates that to a certain extent this has always been the case. Readers have always drawn from literature what is relevant to their own lives and placed their own interpretations upon it. They have always been engaged in a process of self-creation, constructing an identity within the particular parameters of their lives, from the resources available to them, from reading literature and from reading the wider context of their existence. The models for English and creativity that begin in the work of Matthew Arnold and are given more precise shape in the work of Sampson, Hourd and Holbrook, are just that: models. They construct an ideology around creativity and literature that has little to do with what actually happens when people read and even less to do with how they live their lives. As such they are ripe for deconstruction. The real task for the English teacher, though, is one of *re*-construction, a process I believe is given form in Dixon's work and further substance in subsequent work examined below.

Re-construction 1: from critical literacy to a new aesthetic

Critical literacy is an approach to texts that calls on the reader to question and challenge what is presented. As a pedagogical method it expands on the idea of literacy as involving fluency in reading and writing, to one where it encompasses a 'reading' of the wider social context within which representation takes place. As such it seems to offer little to English in terms of creativity. For it tends towards *de*-construction, to breaking down, unmasking and disputation while creativity moves towards building up, making afresh and forging links – to *re*-construction. However, it does bring a much-needed irreverence to the subject; nothing is sacred and everything is contestable. In a sense, then, it leads to a situation in which everything is open to being made afresh, *re*-constructed after all. This is exploited in

Wendy Morgan's (1996) *Critical Literacy in the Classroom: The art of the possible*, which takes as its starting point the premise that critical literacy has a tendency to focus more on theory than practice (viii). She explores ways of reversing this pattern so that theory can productively inform a practice that is both "able to understand something of the complex productive shaping of 'individuals' by ideologies, discourses and practices" (26) and to "develop a different classroom practice, which attempts to engage with the pleasure and desire of teachers and students" (27). She does not engage with the word creativity itself but makes clear reference to processes of making afresh and of transforming existing material. She works with the logic that any theory concerned with how texts are "socially and historically constructed" (1) must contain within it provision for how "they can be reconstructed".

The gap between previous notions of creativity and critical literacy is perhaps one reason why Morgan does not highlight it in this work; tellingly it is to the fore in a book she co-authors a decade later, which explicitly draws attention to "the limitations of critical literacy in terms of its conceptualisations of significant matters such as individual identity, human emotion, and creativity" (Misson and Morgan 2006: x). This subsequent work forges links between critical literacy and 'the aesthetic'. To theory and practice she adds emotion and affect. English does not just involve thinking about and acting upon texts, but about understanding how texts make people *feel* and *react* in particular ways. By extension texts come to have a particular creativity in the way they act on people.

Re-construction 2: creativity and genre

Genre refers to "the different forms texts take with variations in social purpose" (Cope and Kalantzis 1993: 7). A *genre-based* approach to English developed in response to the liberal progressivism of the 1970s and 1980s as an attempt to give more direction to students in how to access and use language without resorting to authoritarian notions of correctness and formality. It shares some of the ideological aims of critical literacy in wanting to provide learners with "access to certain realms of social action and interaction, certain realms of social influence and power". It does this by guiding them in the importance of using particular forms of language in particular situations. Like critical literacy it initially seems to offer little to English in terms of creativity. Criticism of the approach might suggest that it is "underpinned by a more traditional, authoritarian ideology that inducts students into given forms of writing and enforces submission to them" (Morgan 1996: 19). This applies primarily to a genre approach, such as one promoted by J. R. Martin (1989), that seeks to identify dominant 'text types' used in schools and base the teaching of literacy around students learning to recognise the linguistic features of these texts in order to reproduce them.

Alternative versions of a genre-based approach, however, take a more complex, nuanced view and actively promote its potential for creativity. Gunther Kress (1993, 1995) encourages the use of genre to empower students in understanding how to use language in particular contexts, but is wary of simply directing them to reproduce dominant norms of discourse. He emphasises that the approach has "possibilities for change, innovation and creativity – that is, the possibilities and means of altering generic form" (1993: 28). Creativity is thus associated with the transformation of texts and with "linguistic plurality, diversity and difference" (29), qualities that Kress regards as constituting "one of the most productive reservoirs and resources for cultural (and consequently social, political, economic) innovation" (29).

In this view of genre, creativity is both a transformative quality that can actively be encouraged in classrooms and also a feature of language as it is used in social interaction. The former is a central theme of Kress's 1995 manifesto on English teaching, *Writing the Future: English and the making of a culture of innovation*, which explores "the part which the English curriculum can, should and must play in the making of social futures" (1). This involves providing a future-orientated curriculum which sees "the people who experience it, as *making and shaping* that future through their competent and confident action" (3). The latter offers a dialogic view of language that stresses not just the need to recognise that all language use is situated within particular generic conventions, but how these conventions can be played with and manipulated in order to generate new meaning and ways of being.

Re-construction 3: multimodality

Multimodality refers to the way meaning is produced using combinations of 'modes', or systems of communication. It "focuses on modes of representation much broader than language alone" (Cope and Kalantzis 2000: 5) and challenges assumptions about language being the dominant mode of communication. English practitioners (New London Group 1996; Cope and Kalantzis 2000; Kress 2000, 2003, 2010; Kress *et al.* 2005) began expressing an interest in multimodality – alongside 'multiliteracies', a less frequently used term – as a response to opportunities for representation opened up by new digital technologies. To ignore these possibilities and stubbornly maintain a focus almost exclusively on spoken and written modes is an "authoritarian" (Cope and Kalantzis 2000: 5) approach that denies the possibilities for creativity located in the way modes "differ according to culture and context, and have specific cognitive, cultural and social effects" (5). Such difference means that when modes are used in combination new possibilities for meaning come into being, with "multifarious combinations of modes of meaning cutting across boundaries of convention and creating new conventions" (New London Group 1996).

Discussions of multimodality are often accompanied by calls for an increased focus on the production rather than the reception of texts in the classroom. Creativity is transferred away from the material for classroom exploration into the hands of students themselves. New technologies mean they can film as readily as watch, print as readily as read and record as readily as listen. The borderline plagiaristic practices of contemporary cultural production, of *sampling*, *cutting and pasting, mashing, downloading* and *mixing* (Kress 2010: 24) point towards the multiple ways in which it is possible to re-create existing cultural materials so that the first consideration in responding to a text need no longer be about what it means but instead can focus on the particular mode in which a response is to be fixed (94).

The focus on the creativity that learners can impose on materials rather than on what those materials tell them is present in other approaches too. As long ago as 1983, Eagleton proposes a form of 'rhetoric' as an alternative to the models of literary study he so comprehensively deconstructs, in which "what might prove . . . useful will not be the criticism or enjoyment of other people's discourse but the production of one's own" (185). Andrews (2001), also promoting rhetoric, argues that teaching should enable each student "to become a more creative maker of language and manager of communication" (146) in an age when "[k]nowing about language is one thing; but using it, making it and critiquing it are likely to be more essential features of the use of language in the first years of the present century". An essay entitled "The Future of English" (Cliff Hodges, Moss and Shreeve 2000) states that the subject is "[f]or setting in motion independently or collaboratively, capacities for communication; exploration; empathy; imagination; linguistic performance; learning about processes; creative meaning-making" (4). And in some university English departments traditional methods of assessing critical essays have been replaced by a requirement for *re-creative* or *transformative* writing (Knights and Thurgar-Dawson 2006), a move replicated by several exam boards in specifications relating to elements of A-level literature coursework.

Conclusion

In just under a century the relationship between English and creativity has been turned on its head (see Box 1.1). Where once creativity was seen as lying in the hands of a few great writers capable of giving the rest of us an insight into a 'true' existence, it now offers a way of describing the transformative processes by which

---

BOX 1.1 The changing nature of creativity

Creativity in English *was* . . .	Creativity in English *is* . . .
In the hands of the author	In the hands of the reader
Original	Transformative
Internally focused	Externally focused
Fixed	Fluid
Elitist	Democratic
Mystical	Practical
Individual	Dialogic
Monomodal	Multimodal

anyone can work with existing materials in order to bring new meaning into being. Paradoxically much of the subject's content remains the same. Poetry may no longer be a substitute for the creativity of a divine being, but it is still very much part of the school curriculum, as is a whole range of literature, along with a focus on the written word in general. This book has no issue with the continuing presence of the subject's traditional staples and in the majority of chapters explores their relationship to learning and creativity. However, it does so with an awareness that English is also so much more and that it should seek continually to expand its horizons. To do so need not risk leading the subject down a path where its own existence is called into question; rather it is to reinvigorate it as an educational space in which young people can learn to shape and bring meaning to their worlds, through utilising the creativity at their disposal in language and other modes of communication, and through learning how to understand the sources of creativity acting upon them.

Key texts

Cope, B. and Kalantzis, M. (1993) *The powers of literacy: A genre approach to teaching writing*. Pittsburgh, PA: University of Pittsburgh Press.

Cope, B. and Kalantzis, M. (eds) (2000) *Multiliteracies: Literacy learning and the design of social futures*. London and New York: Routledge.

Dixon, J. (1975) *Growth through English: Set in the perspective of the seventies*. Huddersfield: NATE.

Hourd, M.L. (1949) *The education of the poetic spirit: A study in children's expression in the English lesson*. London: William Heinemann Ltd.

Morgan, W. (1996) *Critical literacy in the classroom: The art of the possible*. London and New York: Routledge.

Sampson, G. (1922) *English for the English: A chapter on national education*. Cambridge: Cambridge University Press.

2

Theories of creativity, English and learning

> The mind does something else: it creates. It thinks of things which are not 'out there', in the world. Things which *could not* be out there in the world. The mind thinks, it creates, it imagines.
>
> Steven Mithen, *The Prehistory of the Mind*

The uses to which creativity can be put are so diverse (Banaji and Burn 2008) that any attempt to apply it to more than one term – in other words, to English *and* to learning – is fraught with complication. A wealth of material exists linking creativity to both fields, so that English, for example, can draw on work that explores the creativity of language (Volosinov 2000; Carter 2004; Bakhtin 2006), of literary writing (Kearney 1988, 2002; Attridge 2004) and of forms of representation and meaning-making in general (Cope and Kalantzis 2000; Kress 2000), while learning can refer to a range of official documents (NACCCE 1999; QCA 2005; Safford and Barrs 2005; Roberts 2006; Ofsted 2010) as well as academic studies promoting and exploring the pedagogical value of creativity (Gardner 1993; Craft, Jeffrey and Leibling 2001; Craft 2005; Beghetto and Kaufman 2010; Starko 2010). The word creativity may occur in all these works and be the central focus of most of them, but this does not mean that the different ideas presented are easily reconciled to form a coherent account of creativity, English *and* learning. The opposite is the case. For creativity has as many meanings as fields to which it applies. It is perhaps more useful to think in terms of *creativities* than *creativity*.

Rather than focus on how theories of *creativity and learning* link to English this book focuses on how theories of *creativity and English* link to learning. This may seem little more than a semantic point, but it is not done simply to navigate a way through the wealth of critical material available; instead, it serves to draw attention to the distinctive links between English and creativity. For unlike many subjects, English's engagement with creativity lies not just in adopting particular pedagogical approaches, but in the very material of study. And while other subjects categorised under the banner of 'the creative arts' can make similar claims, English is unique in the opportunities it has to exploit the creativity of language. Particular pedagogical approaches generic to many subject areas and embodied in phrases such as "teaching for creativity" (NACCCE 1999) and "creative learning" (Jeffrey and Craft 2003) are drawn on throughout the book, but the main focus is on how the creativity of English offers its own route to learning. Consequently the bulk of this chapter explores the relationship between creativity and English, not in the specific way it has manifested itself in particular classroom practices over time, but in how creativity is theorised in relation to the subject's main concerns. It begins by exploring the links between language, creativity and human development in general, before examining the creativity of language as it relates to ways of thinking and social engagement and then moving on to a consideration of the special case that can be made for the creativity of literary writing. It then explains why we might talk in terms of 'ordinary creativity' before offering a summary of the types of learning that emerge when focusing on English and creativity.

Evolutionary creativity

Early humans, living between six million and one hundred thousand years ago (Mithen 1996: 21), did not possess qualities readily identifiable as creative. This can be demonstrated by a visit to the British Museum to view its oldest human artefact, a hand-axe, dated as being over one million years old. Gazing on the object, one can't but wonder at the ingenuity that brought it into being. However, the wonder is dampened when other examples of hand-axes designed over the next million years or so are considered. They are almost identical. It seems that there was no development of basic hand-axe design or the introduction of any other tools until much more recent times.

Clearly Early Humans were not given the lesson objective: improve the effectiveness and versatility of hand-axes (by, for example, adding a wooden handle). Developments were impossible because their minds were unable to conceive of them. They were not human as we exist today. Only with an evolutionary shift in the way the mind works, occurring approximately one hundred thousand years ago (Mithen 1996; Tomasello 1999) were humans able to create new tools and, indeed, to create cultural artefacts of any kind. Something happened which meant that humans could work on the materiality of their existence, shape it, change it, speculate on it. Something gave them the potential for creativity.

We can only conjecture as to how and why the shift occurred. Two contrasting theories have significance for creativity and English. The first, from evolutionary archaeologist Stephen Mithen (1996), in *The Prehistory of the Mind: A search for the origins of art, religion and science*, theorises that the minds of Modern Humans (*Homo Sapiens Sapiens*) developed 'cognitive fluidity'. 'Modules' in the mind, he suggests, stopped operating separately to carry out discrete functions and began to work together, enabling knowledge not only to be stored in the mind, but also to be acted upon and re-presented in multiple fashions through such processes as analogy, projection, symbolisation, reflexivity and "an almost limitless capacity for imagination" (77). Above all, cognitive fluidity made possible sophisticated language use: from now on humans could develop the hand-axe because they could not only conceive of different models, but they could articulate and speculate on what they might look like. "As a result," writes Mithen, "the whole of human behaviour was pervaded with the flexibility and creativity that is characteristic of Modern Humans" (219).

A second theorist, evolutionary psychologist Michel Tomasello (1999), rejects a modular view of the mind. Instead he ascribes human cognitive development to language itself, claiming that "the process of acquiring and using linguistic symbols fundamentally transforms the nature of human cognitive representation" (123). In other words cognitive fluidity comes from the mind's ability to use symbolic language rather than the structure of the mind itself. Once humans have a symbolic system of language available then they are able to project multiple perspectives on to the world. In simple terms, a dog might also be an animal, a pet or a pest and a single place might be described as the beach, the shore, the coast or the sand (8). Such "perspectivally based cognitive representations" have significant implications for human development, freeing people from communication based on direct sensory experience and instead "enabling multiple simultaneous representations of each and every, indeed all possible, perceptual situations". This ability to explore the possible, in other words to imagine alternatives and hold them in the mind, or fix them in time by putting them into words, might usefully be labelled creativity. It gives humans the potential to push against existing forms in a system of "tension between doing things conventionally, which has many obvious advantages, and doing things creatively, which has its own advantages as well" (53). Language gives humans the ability to preserve and pass on knowledge, but also to work on, develop, transform, or even reject that knowledge.

The creativity of language does not just lie in its moment of articulation, but in the opportunities it offers for the further and continuous development of alternative possibilities. In the way it allows knowledge to be stored in the mind and re-articulated at a later date (with further options brought about by the 'invention' of writing), it operates a kind of "ratchet effect" (5) that means modifications can be made to the cultural traditions and artefacts of human beings over time without being lost. They are both preserved in and transformed by language in a process of "cumulative cultural evolution" (4). Consequently human development takes place in historical rather than evolutionary time (Dawkins 1989 [1976]; Mithen 1996; Sperber 1996; Blackmore 1999; Tomasello 1999). Advances in human achievement outstrip the potential for evolutionary change by many millennia, giving us the unique "power to turn against our creators" (Dawkins 1989 [1976]: 201). English teachers sceptical of the relevance of this material to their subject might pause to consider the speed with which change occurs. The language of Chaucer is separated from that of today by a mere twenty or so generations, each perfectly able to communicate with the next, yet a huge transformation is present in the cumulative gap (189). English as a subject dealing with language and language change clearly has a part to play in this dual process of continuation and change. The cultural and linguistic shifts that take place over centuries and millennia can be mirrored in microcosm within the individual journey of a learner, encouraged to work on his or her own language, while also aware of the capacity for language to preserve and transmit. Thinking about "creativity over the long term" (Hodder 1998: 64) also fosters an awareness of it not necessarily lying in a particular action, or in a moment of inspiration, or within the mind of a particular individual. It exists in all that has gone before, and in the potential of all that is to come. Creativity, in this sense, is a very lengthy process of construction indeed, much like learning itself.

Linguistic creativity

Human cultural evolution does not depend on the creativity of language *per se*, but on the creativity of language as it emerges in social use. Works that stress the dialogic nature of language explain that it is not simply a medium for transmitting knowledge, but the means by which knowledge is constructed in social interaction (Volosinov 2000; Bakhtin 2006) and in the relationship between language and thought (Vygotsky 1986 [1936]). Creativity, then, is forged in dialogue, so that what is uttered by one person is received, processed and transformed by another, or by the speaker's own internal voice. This requires consideration not just of words as they are exchanged but of the cognitive processing that results in transformation. We carry out such processing every time we hear or read a word – or, indeed, hear or see anything. It is at the core of how the mind works both to create and to learn. Whether it is forged in the way the mind is structured, or the way language acts on the mind, is, in a sense, unimportant. What is important is that something happens.

Vygotsky and creativity in the mind

Russian psychologist Lev Vygotsky (1986 [1936]) offers a theory of how language and thought work dialogically in a process of "continual movement back and forth from thought to word and from word to thought" (218). In his model "thought is not merely expressed in words; it comes into existence through them". The 'inner speech' of thought does not consist of actual words, but can only take on meaning, be created, if transferred as words into the realm of 'outer speech'. When externalised, language is able, once again, to act on thought, to generate additional meanings, link words to other words and tease out alternative significance so that "every thought tends to connect something with something else, to establish a relation between things" (218).

Vygotsky explains that "inner speech" functions not as "speech minus sound, but as an entirely separate speech function" (235) and that while "outer speech" begins with words, building up to sentences and whole texts, inner speech starts with the whole but is capable of reducing complex thoughts down to a single word. Thus the entire plot of Shakespeare's *Hamlet* – as well as the multiple ideas that surround it – can be held in the mind as its single word title (247). If you want to feel how this works, take a moment to imagine everything you have done today. Multiple recollections should flood your mind, even though you can hold them all under the single word 'today'. Yet if you were to explain your day to a friend you would have to transform the one word into many. You would also have to make choices about what to include and miss out and about the particularities of your vocabulary. "A thought," says Vygotsky rather poetically for a theoretical psychologist, "may be compared to a cloud shedding a shower of words" (251). Put more prosaically, a thought contains creative potential, realised in words. Concurrently, however, words possess the same potential when transferred to the realm of thought. Each word is a cloud capable of stimulating many thoughts. This two-way process is particularly important for teachers to consider because it suggests the quality of language input received by students affects the quality of their own output. It stimulates thought and thought stimulates language. The more complex the language, the more complex the possible thoughts; the more complex the thoughts, the more language must be relied upon to adequately translate those thoughts. Language, then, is not just the medium through which students learn, but is a prerequisite for how well they are able to learn. At least two leading theorists (Williams 1977: 43; Armstrong 2000: 137) see Vygotsky's insight into language as being so compelling because of a willingness to recognise it as both constitutive and constituting. In other words, language makes us human, but we can make something of our humanity through the way we use language. Such a view helps teachers to justify using creativity in their lessons on two fronts: because it is part of who we are and because it helps us develop towards who we are to become. This model of the relationship between thought and language will be returned to and expanded upon several times in the course of this book because of the implications it has for how learning is advanced both by the processing action of the mind and by external social forces acting upon it.

Volosinov and dialogic creativity

If Vygotsky helps us to understand the creative capacity of the mind as it interacts with the social world as expressed in language, then his contemporary and compatriot, Valentin Volosinov (2000) offers an interesting perspective on the creativity of language itself, how it is constantly acted on and transformed in dialogic, social interaction to the point where "dialogue assumes the character of a primordial source of social creativity in general" (translator's note: 4, in Vygotsky 2000).

Volosinov sees words as existing in a "chain of ideological creativity" (11), so that their denotation can never be fixed, but is always contingent on "their new contextual meaning" (77). Thus the very process of using a word is creative, part of "a ceaseless flow of becoming" (66). Creativity lies not in the word itself but in the meaning activated in the context of a particular utterance. Without context, words are empty of meaning. Used in an utterance, they take on meaning in relation to other words and in the particulars of the moment of use. Like Vygotsky, he distinguishes between "the process of inner and outer verbal life" (96) but his concern is more with how words come to take on particular meanings in actual use than with how they are processed in the mind. Thus he structures all language use as in response to other language use. This involves trying to comprehend what has been said with recourse to one's own linguistic resources, so that "[u]nderstanding strives to match the speaker's words with a *counter word*" (102). The dialogic process clearly operates on two planes in this formulation. There is the dialogue between speakers, with meaning being created according to the various responses each give out and receive, and there is the dialogue of the individual, as the word interacts with his or her own experience and linguistic resources.

The paradoxical nature of language as conceived by Volosinov – that it carries meaning yet without dialogue is empty of meaning – is key to thinking about its use in an approach to English that focuses on creativity. It highlights the need for all language study to be clearly situated within a particular context. Without context, dialogic engagement is impossible, words deprived of their potential for meaning. The more complete the context, the more complete the meaning, for students are able to situate words in a way that considers multiple possibilities for variation.

Bakhtin and the creativity of whole forms

Volosinov's work allows us to consider the creativity of language as it demands a response. Each response generates new meaning by re-situating words, no matter how small the shift in context. Language, as constituted here, is dynamic, not so much a carrier as a generator of meaning. Another Russian, Mikhail Bakhtin (2006), places limits on this proliferation of meaning. For while each 'utterance' is made in a modified social context to the previous one, it is bound by the conventions of 'speech genres', which "organize our speech in almost the same way as grammatical (syntactical) forms do" (78). Effectively, all language is bound by particular codes of use. Without these codes, possibilities for meaning would be restricted. For readers and listeners would have a limited indication of the context within which a word is used.

To say simply that Volosinov illustrates the creativity of language while Bakhtin shows how this creativity is held within bounds, however, is to misunderstand the work of both. For Volosinov's "chain of ideological creativity" (2000: 11) is just that: a *chain*. New meaning may be created each time a word is used in dialogue, but it is always connected in some way to previous meanings. And in commenting on how 'speech genres' help organise utterances into a coherent, meaningful form, Bakhtin is not suggesting that they are fixed or are not, in turn, open to generating creativity and being used creatively. It is simply that such creativity cannot occur until a genre is firmly established and is thoroughly understood by its users, for ". . . to use a genre freely and creatively is not the same as to create a genre from the beginning; genres must be fully mastered in order to be manipulated freely" (80).

Freire, dialogic creativity and agency

Brazilian educationalist Paulo Freire (1996 [1970]) extends our comprehension of the approaches of Vygotsky, Volosinov and Bakhtin by exploring how an understanding of the dialogic nature of language can lead to a critical and creative engagement with the world, one which promotes possibilities for human agency and the transformation of one's social existence.

Freire's celebrated *Pedagogy of the Oppressed* (1996 [1970]), based on his own work with Brazilian peasants in the 1960s, outlines how traditional, transmission models of teaching, what he calls "the banking concept of education" (53), reinforce social hierarchies by "depositing" information held by those in authority into the minds of passive recipients. He calls instead for a "problem-posing method of education" (62) in which students are "no longer docile listeners" but "critical co-investigators in dialogue with the teacher". The method involves teachers presenting material to students for them to consider; the teacher then re-considers his or her own initial position as students express their own. Thus teachers and students work on material in a process of co-creation. Freire is insistent on the need for people to work on the material presented to them so that as they transform it they also transform themselves in a continual "process of *becoming*" (64). "Authentic" existence occurs only when people are "engaged in inquiry and creative transformation".

There is no intention to draw direct parallels between the oppressed Brazilian peasants of several decades ago and students in English classrooms today. However, as teachers, it is worth constantly reminding ourselves that education has the potential to inhibit creativity and learning as well as to nourish it, and that the way we structure our lessons and ourselves within those lessons is important if we are to encourage young people to strive to *become* rather than just *be*. The point is all the more powerful when wrapped up in Freire's invigorating language, whereby "[k]nowledge emerges only through invention and re-invention, through the restless, impatient, continuing, hopeful inquiry human beings pursue in the world, with the world, and with each other" (53).

As *Pedagogy of the Oppressed* continues, Freire moves on from exploring the teacher–student relationship to looking at the role of language in this relationship, particularly dialogue and "the essence of dialogue itself: *the word*" (68). He presents us with a model of 'the word' which sees it as a site for continual creativity, simultaneously reflected and acted upon in any dialogic exchange. The reflection comes from the way the word is received and the thoughts it inspires in use; the action comes from the way the word is used and re-used, modified, no matter how slightly, to fit the world of the user, but in the process modifying in some way the world of the receiver. Reflecting and acting on words (engaging in what Freire calls "praxis") is thus acting on worlds; "to speak a true word," Freire explains, "is to transform the world" (68). Freire's work makes explicit the possibilities for learning opened up when students engage with their own worlds at the point where they interact with new worlds brought into the classroom. When done effectively, new knowledge and ways of seeing and being come about: "the naming of the world [becomes] an act of creation and re-creation" (70).

Literary creativity

Creativity largely disappears as a topic for academic literary discourse in the final three decades of the twentieth century (Pope 2005: 7). It is easy to see why. Radical new theories broadly labelled as structuralism (Culler 1975) and poststructuralism or deconstruction (Culler 1982) strip literature of its special aura and unmask the ideas of previous generations as being based on false premises. Artists from the Romantic period onwards may claim to be replacing God as a source of creativity and authenticity in response to the alienating forces of industry and commerce (Pope 2005: 39), but their work, it transpires, does not spring from souls more sensitive than those of the rest of us or even from their own intentions; it is constructed from the social forces acting upon them and so reflects the values of its time rather than a core, timeless humanity. Not only are authors no longer 'creators', they are to all intents and purposes removed from academic literary discourse altogether, declared as dead (Barthes 1977).

One strand of literary thinking in this period does hold out new possibilities for creativity. Reader response theory (Iser 1978; Fish 1990) shifts attention away from trying to find out the core meaning of texts – their *essential* creativity – to exploring a range of available meanings based on the position of the reader. Thus texts are permanently in a state of becoming rather than of being, as each new reading brings with it new possibilities. While it focuses on multiple perspectives and alternative meanings, tellingly it makes little reference to creativity. Perhaps the connotations of the word are still tied up too closely with ideas of the author as a divine-like presence. For reader-response theory develops as part of a move to disrupt elitist notions of literature. If meaning is constructed by the reader, then anyone can make a valid attempt at reading any work; by extension, any text becomes valid material for study. Meaning can be ascribed to the text on the back of a cereal packet as legitimately as to *War and Peace*.

In recent years creativity and related ideas, such as the aesthetic, the imagination and story-telling, have re-emerged as topics worthy of consideration in academic literary discourse (Kearney 1988, 2002; Armstrong 2000; Attridge 2004; Pope 2005; Misson and Morgan 2006, 2007). In part this is a reaction to "culturally impoverishing and politically disabling" (Armstrong 2000: 2) deconstructive theories that tend to pull apart objects for analysis without remaking them. It is also an attempt to build "a poetics of the possible" (Kearney 1988: 32), to recognise that some ways of being and of doing, exemplified in particular ways of using language, may well offer insight into what it means to be human in ways that resist deconstruction. This offers hope for the at-times beleaguered proponents of the value of literature in the curriculum. If it is to be taught in a meaningful way – to engage, motivate and aid learning – then it needs to be presented not just as material upon which to impose a response, but also as material that can stimulate particular kinds of response, in ways that no other material can. Attention needs to be drawn to its transactional potential (Rosenblatt 1978), its ability to work upon people as they, in turn, work upon it. The inclusion here of a section on 'literary creativity' marks a belief in opportunities for learning in literature that are not necessarily present in other forms: for literature is born out of conscious attempts at linguistic creativity which in turn promote particular kinds of creative response.

Separating literary from linguistic creativity

Bakhtin (2006) makes a special case for the creativity of 'artistic literature' over other forms of language use when he asserts that its "individual style enters directly into the very task of the utterance" (63). Its conventions actively demand that writers seek to move beyond generic constraints and so its very essence relies upon creativity and transformation. Bakhtin's focus on the dialogic nature of language means that the creativity of literary texts comes from two sources: there is the creativity of the language as it affects readers and the creativity of readers as they process the language. A literary text is richer in generative potential than others because it is more likely to use vocabulary and structure in ways that readers have not met before; consequently it imposes a greater range of meanings on readers who, in turn, have more material from which to create their own meanings.

Bakhtin, though, pays little attention to the content of literature – to narrative, or story. His focus is on the linguistic rather than the literary. It is only with the introduction of story, I would argue, that a more definitive case can be made for the creativity of literature, one that can be used to justify its prominence in the secondary school curriculum, and goes beyond seeing it as special just because it is written in a particular way. To this end, story might usefully be conceived of as a third party in the middle of the dialogical exchange between text and reader. In this position, it is both *complete*, in the sense that it is a created whole, attempting to present a particular view of the world, and *incomplete*, in that it is always being worked upon by the writer and the reader in order to understand that particular world and relate it to their own worlds. It is both of the text and of the reader, but also beyond them, a touchstone for something possible but also out of reach, for something real yet imagined. Kearney (2002: 151) explains how stories are linked to human agency in the way that they all come from real life and yet indelibly alter real life by bringing something else into being. Thus when we read a story the language acts upon us and we act upon the language, but the story as a whole also has a role to play. Even though a creation, it references actual events to which it relates in some way or another, the action of real life, and, once read, it is fed back into the action of real life through the changed perceptions of the reader. Consequently a story is not an "ethically neutral" (156) space to which the reader brings his or her ideas; rather "each story seeks to persuade us one way or another about the evaluative character of its actors and their actions". We do not have to accept what the text is trying to do to us as we read, but cannot ignore the fact that an attempt is being made in the first place. Thus we might ostensibly be in control of interpreting a story, but "this is only up to a certain point". The fact remains that the story dictates *what* we respond to, and so must be implicated in some way in the creativity it generates. The author must play a role too. He or she may well have no control over how, when or where the work is read, but will consciously have created it within the context of certain generic, literary conventions, and so have imposed some fixity in possible responses. Kearney summarises this perspective in a way that makes it clear that the creativity of a literary text lies in multiple origins, each inseparable from the other:

> The story is not confined to the mind of the author alone (the romantic fallacy regarding the primacy of the author's original intentions). Nor is it confined to the mind of its reader. Nor indeed to the action of its narrated actors. Every story is a play of at least three persons (author/actor/addressee) whose outcome is never final. That is why narrative is an open-ended invitation to ethical and poetic responsiveness. Storytelling invites us to become not just agents of our own lives, but narrators and readers as well. It shows us that the untold life is not worth living.
>
> (156)

Aesthetics and literary creativity

The disappearance of creativity from academic literary discourse is accompanied by a similar diminution in the status of related terms, perhaps most notably 'the aesthetic', which is defined in the dictionary as "concerned with beauty or the appreciation of beauty" and as "rejecting the notion that art should have a social or moral purpose". However, such definitions are misleading, drawn from literary and artistic movements of the late nineteenth century that actively seek to distance art from real life. For 'the aesthetic' also captures the *experience* of art and only focuses on beauty at the expense of actual life if art is assigned such a function. Thus when Dewey's (2005 [1934]) *Art as Experience* develops a radical theory of art as "a process of doing and making" (48) it links the aesthetic to "actual life-experience" (1) so that it is received not in a spirit of refined detachment, but "framed for enjoyed, receptive perception" (49). Dewey argues that the consumption of art, "esthetics", is as important as its production, suggesting that art is not just born of experience but *is* an experience in itself. Consequently *understanding* a work of art is inseparable from *feeling* the work of art. This requires, in Dewey's terms, that "a beholder must *create* his own experience" (56) in a way that replicates "the process of organization the creator of the work consciously experienced". Just as "[t]he artist selected, simplified, clarified, abridged and condensed according to [his] interest", so "the beholder must go through these operations according to his point of view and interest" in "an act of recreation".

Isobel Armstrong's (2000) *The Radical Aesthetic* borrows from Dewey in seeking to develop "a democratic aesthetic" (2) in response to a dominant orthodoxy of anti-aestheticism. She calls on us to broaden "the scope of what we think of as art", in order to understand the particular role it plays in our lives. In doing so she offers a theory that links "the components of aesthetic life" with "those that are already embedded in the processes and practices of consciousness". She identifies a special place for the aesthetic in life, but also recognises it as being an ordinary, everyday activity. Thus the four components of her study are "experiences that keep us alive

. . . playing and dreaming, thinking and feeling" (2). Her focus is very much on *what art can do*, as well as *what we can do to art*. Such a configuration opens up new possibilities for how literature is used in the classroom. Its creativity can be played with in ways that bring about further creativity. Playful and sensible responses, far-fetched and grounded approaches, rational and emotional reactions all have legitimacy and value.

Literary encounters with alterity

If I read an instruction manual, I may well learn something: how to put up a set of shelves, for example. However, there is no creativity involved in this learning, just a simple transmission of knowledge. A literary text serves a different function and so offers a different relationship to learning. It brings into being 'possible worlds' that demand comparison with actual ones. No matter how close to the actual world of the reader, the literary work is 'other', an alternative perspective in contrast to existing configurations of knowledge. Attridge (2004) uses the phrase "an encounter with alterity" (46) to describe the experience of meeting something from outside one's own experience in a literary work. The word "encounter" suggests the dynamic nature of the experience: it works on the reader, gives him or her a new perspective, but is also worked on by the reader, created in the meeting point of the actual and the possible. Creativity here comes not just from meeting something new, but from transforming it as one's own experience is transformed.

Ordinary creativity and making meaning

Labelling creativity as ordinary is not meant to diminish its effect; rather it is to view it as essential to the practice of everyday life. Or at least of a full and worth-while life. For creativity exists in the possibilities of existence, in the to-and-fro of human interaction, in the way we use language, in the way culture helps us to explain our lives, in our desire for enquiry and in our thirst for knowledge. It is there in our quest to push back boundaries, to break the mould and to do as well as we can. It is there in any form of learning that springs from our own desires and impulses and that involves us actively engaging with the world rather than passively accepting it. Psychoanalyst D. W. Winnicott (1971: 69) explains how such active engagement is equally present "in the moment-by-moment living of a backward child who is enjoying breathing as it is in the inspiration of an architect who suddenly knows what it is that he wishes to construct". This is because both are using the materials available to them to bring shape and meaning to the world as best they can, thus stating their presence to those around them. In ways big and small, they are transforming the world. To Winnicott (65), it is this "creative apperception more than anything else that makes the individual feel that life is worth living". His justification for such a statement lies in how he positions people in relation to "external reality". Creativity involves working on this reality, transforming it in some way; thus an individual's relationship with the world can be one of constant becoming and involvement. "Contrasted with this," he continues,

> is a relationship to external reality which is one of compliance, the world and its details being recognised but only as something to be fitted in with or demanding adaptation . . .. In some ways or other our theory includes a belief that living creatively is a healthy state, and that compliance is a sick basis for society.

I do not think it is too far-fetched a notion to see English as having the potential to contribute to healthy states of existence. For the very materials of the subject are those that bring shape and meaning to existence, that help people impose themselves on external reality.

Ordinary creativity has the potential to be present in all areas of human expression, be they casual, everyday exchanges, such as gossip and general chat (Carter 2004), or great artistic works. And to say, as in the previous section, that creativity exists in responses to great works as much as in the works themselves is neither to trivialise great artistic creations, nor to exaggerate the impact of responses; for viewing creativity as ordinary allows for due consideration of what occurs in all creative interactions. They are not moments that, realistically, are going to result in a fundamental shift in perspectives, but they are moments that move life along, that change its co-ordinates, no matter how minutely. And perhaps that is another way in which creativity links to learning, particularly in English. For evidence of learning – in spite of what is demanded by many school inspection regimes – can take time to emerge. But that does not mean that learning is not taking place. When viewed as a process (Apple 2004; Kelly 2009), learning is part of an ordinary, ongoing engagement with life, one that is active and creative, but not necessarily responsive in set, measurable ways to particular stimuli.

Defining creativity as ordinary is also not to suggest that it occurs in all situations at all times. Winnicott's healthy existence is perhaps more easily squashed than sustained. For example, classroom life is artificial and often more readily focused on control and containment than expression and discovery. Ironically classrooms that impose restrictions often have the opposite effect, with students displaying a "symbolic creativity" (Willis 1990) both in and out of school in the form of defiant behaviour and alternative youth cultures. This book wants to avoid pushing such creativity to the margins by fostering a sense of co-operative creativity within the classroom, one where students are learning from new material and ideas but at the same time where their own interests and views are valued and explored within the context of study. Such an approach lays itself open to charges of being unrealistic and excessively utopian. However, I prefer to see it as an attempt to aid students in a process of self-creation. In the interplay of what students know and believe with what they do not know or have experience of comes both creativity and learning. To deny either is to limit human potential.

Conclusion

This chapter began by explaining its focus on how theories of *creativity and English* link to learning rather than how theories of *creativity and learning* link to English. The approach grew out of the difficulties faced in trying to bring together aspects of all three fields: creativity, English *and* learning. However, reading through the chapter it is clear that many of the processes by which creativity is activated in English and acts upon English are the same ones by which learning takes place. Creativity *in* English, for example, relies on transformation, dialogic interaction, context, extended processes and challenges to dominant norms, just as learning does. We have reached a state of affairs where creativity and learning both represent a 'normal' state of being. They are both 'ordinary', in the sense that our impulse, when freed from restriction, is to create, is to learn.

Below is a summary of various forms of English that might usefully be referred to when considering how and why creativity is integral to learning in the subject.

Transformative English

Creativity is a transformative process. It acts on existing materials to bring something new into being. It thus mirrors learning, which involves the transformation of existing knowledge into new and extended forms. English is well placed to explore this link. Helping students become confident in the use of language and other modes of communication, enables them to learn through experimenting with different ways of being and gives them the potential to transform the conditions of their own existence.

Dialogic English

English, in its primary concern with language, but also with other modes of communication, is a key site for the dialogic interaction that is important to creativity and learning. Dialogue generates meaning and so is, in itself, a creative process. Learning takes place in the cognitive engagement that each shift in meaning brings about, but also in reflecting on various possibilities for meaning brought about through dialogue.

Situated English

Creativity and learning cannot take place in a vacuum, but need to be situated in a context that allows for a full and proper understanding of any material engaged with. Learning can be situated in past experience or in offering full, stimulating access to new materials. In both cases creativity and learning occur in the new meaning brought into being when what is already known and what is not known come into contact. Understanding of context increases alongside one's competence in using and understanding language. The greater one's language capabilities, the greater the connections one can draw from a particular word in a particular context, the greater the variety of meanings one can place on it.

Process-based English

Creativity and learning take place over time. They involve becoming rather than being. In developing language use, encouraging experimentation with different forms of representation and providing exposure to a range of texts, English provides models for ways of becoming. It shows how meaning is always being extended, generated afresh, and so encourages learners to consider and take control of the processes of creativity and learning.

Healthy English

Creativity and learning both require challenging what is already known in order to generate fresh knowledge and ways of looking at the world. This calls for a healthy form of non-compliance whereby learners are given the opportunity, if they wish, to reject knowledge as it is presented to them and to create it afresh in forms suitable to their own purposes. Such an approach refuses a model of education that sees students as passively receiving instruction and calls instead for them to bring their own creativity to materials. It is not a rejection of knowledge *per se*, but of particular ways of presenting knowledge. English, with its focus on the representational qualities of language and other modes of communication, is the means by which students can have control and understanding of any healthy non-compliance.

Ordinary English

Language is a function of everyday life. The limits of our language dictate, in many ways, the limits of our existence, or at least possible existence, our ability to project beyond our present confines to an imagined alternative. This is not necessarily born out of a desire to escape our current existence, but out of the ordinary quality of seeking to move on, to learn new things, to create. All learning is situated in the notion that it is something, as humans, we instinctively do. By extension we instinctively create, in that we constantly strive to use and make sense of the materials at our disposal. English not only deals with these materials, but allows for extended thinking and learning in reflecting on and studying the ongoing impact of what is created through them.

Key texts

Attridge, D. (2004) *The singularity of literature*. London and New York: Routledge.
Bakhtin, M. (2006) *Speech genres and other late essays*. Austin, TX: University of Texas Press.
Kearney, R. (1988) *The wake of imagination: Ideas of creativity in Western culture*. London: Hutchinson Education.

Mithen, S. (1996) *The prehistory of the mind: A search for the origins of art, religion and science*. London: Phoenix Paperback.

Tomasello, M. (1999) *The cultural origins of human cognition*. Cambridge, MA: Harvard University Press.

Volosinov, V. N. (2000) *Marxism and the philosophy of language*. Harvard, MA: Harvard University Press.

Vygotsky, L. (1986) [1936] *Thought and language*. Cambridge, MA and London: The MIT Press.

Part II

Creativity and the English curriculum

3

Creativity, English and modality

The world told is a different world to *the world shown.*

Gunther Kress, *Literacy in the New Media Age*

This chapter's original title referred to media rather than modes, modes being the communication systems by which meaning is generated and received (e.g. writing, music, image), media the forms that incorporate these modes (e.g. books, films, radio). Modality is preferred because it draws attention to the processes by which creativity occurs rather than the physical representations in which it is contained. To give an example, a television programme might be particularly creative, but it is so because of its use of various modes, of image, sound, speech, etc. and the opportunities viewers have to respond to these. Of course, creativity might lie in the particularities of the medium too: for example, the programme's relation to others of its type, scheduling at a particular time of the day, or the way it is promoted. However, perhaps these examples are more at home in the separate realm of Media Studies. A focus on modality, with its close links to creativity and meaning-making (Kress 2010), allows for a more straightforward inclusion of various media into the subject of English. In a sense it provides a solution of sorts to arguments about whether or not English and Media Studies should be subsumed under one subject heading, such as Communication Studies, or Cultural Studies. English explores the way meaning is created in texts (by no means the only thing it does, of course), primarily in the modes that use the word, but in others too; Media Studies explores the production and function of the texts themselves. Such a distinction still leaves fuzzy boundaries between the two, not least because meaning is produced in the choice of medium used for representation as well as the choice of modes. However, while it is commonplace to talk of the language of film (or film literacy), or the language of advertising, both, in fact, contain several languages – or modes. Both involve, to name a few examples, image, diagetic and non-diagetic sound, colour, text and texture. Language itself may be too abstract a term for the discussions that follow. For there are distinct differences in the *modes* of writing and of speaking (Kress 2010).

Perhaps the chapter's title needs adapting further, replacing 'modality' with 'multimodality', for essentially it does not look at modes in isolation but as they interact with and complement one another. The concept of multimodality, developed in English teaching initially as a response to advances in new media technologies democratising modes of production previously inaccessible to all but a privileged few (New London Group 1996; Cope and Kalantzis 2000), offers exciting opportunities for the subject and creativity, enabling an exploration of how meaning can be brought into being and responded to in multiple, combinatory fashions. It also, however, presents the subject with a threat. If proponents of multimodality are to be taken at face value in their argument for a "democratic stance" in which "all modes are equal" then, as English teachers, we must "fundamentally rethink the position of verbal resources within semiotic configurations" (Page 2010: 4). In other words, the subject must no longer privilege writing over other forms of communication, a move that would threaten its very identity. Instead, the written word is one available option among others as to how to receive and generate meaning. Its use must also consider the impact of other modes upon it, even to the extent that writing itself can be seen as multimodal, also incorporating visual design (for example in the choice of font) and the potential for sound.

This chapter stops short of seeing verbal modes, both of speaking and writing, as being neither more nor less important than other forms of communication. Privileging them above others is perhaps a futile exercise, open to criticism about trying to cling on to the past and of denying young people a full engagement with the worlds in which they operate. There is no desire here to hark back to former glories, or to deny students chances to explore and generate meaning in as many ways as is feasibly possible. There is, however, a wish to promote learning and to advance young people in their cognitive capabilities. In this, the chapter suggests, the spoken and written word remains of pre-eminent importance, indispensable to particular forms of creativity that stimulate learning. Such creativity can be further enhanced and taken in new directions by an awareness and use of other modes, but written and spoken language remain at the heart of learning. Thus this chapter embraces a multimodal approach to English but advocates maintaining the study of language as its core. It begins by suggesting why the verbal modes are so important to learning before exploring how they might reposition themselves within the modern multimodal landscape. The examples that follow also show how the visual in particular, but also the aural and other modes, have a role to play in the subject, and how they are sources of creativity both separate to and alongside the verbal.

Re-positioning the verbal

Absolutely English is not and should not be exclusively about exploring verbal modes of communication. To do so restricts creativity and learning, for if these stem from adopting multiple perspectives on the world, then it makes sense to encourage students to derive meaning from a range of modes and, in turn, express their thoughts in similarly diverse forms. This stimulates learning through a process akin to synaesthesia (Kress 2003; Ramachandran 2011), whereby cognitive development comes through the transference of ideas from one mode to another. "It is in the realm of synaesthesia," Kress argues, "that much of what we regard as 'creativity' happens" (36).

Kress is a key figure in understanding the relationship between multimodality and English. He has written extensively on the subject, invariably linking it to calls for greater innovation and creativity (2000, 2003, 2010). His radical perspective claims that the dominant mode is no longer that of the verbal but of the visual and that the shift carries with it "profound effects on human, cognitive/affective, cultural and bodily engagement with the world, and on the forms and shapes of knowledge" (Kress 2003: 1). There is seemingly little to argue with here. If we accept that shifts in cognitive functioning occur with the spread of reading and writing (Wolf 2008), then it seems logical to accept that the ready availability of the visual as a means of 'reading' and 'writing' has a similar impact on how we think. It is worth quoting Kress at length exploring changes in reading to demonstrate his novel and compelling line of argument:

> The current landscape of communication can be characterised by the metaphor of the move from *telling the world* to *showing the world*. The metaphor points to a profound change in the act of reading, which can be characterised by the phrases 'reading as interpreting' and 'reading as ordering'. The metaphor and the two phrases allow us to explore the questions that reading poses – narrowly as 'getting meaning from a written text', and widely as 'making sense of the world around me' – through a new lens. Both senses of reading rest on the idea of *reading as sign-making*. The signs that are made by readers in their reading draw on *what there is to be read*. They draw on the shape of the cultural world of representation, and on the reader's prior training in how and what to read. New forms of reading, when texts *show the world* rather than *tell the world* have consequences for the relations between makers and remakers of meaning (writers and readers, image-makers and viewers).
>
> (2003: 140)

Again, there is seemingly nothing to argue against. Kress's point that in a multimodal world students must learn to read the meaning all around them rather than that simply contained within written text gives new purpose and direction to English teachers taking on his ideas: our subject really does lie at the heart of understanding and, in turn, re-making the world.

There is one area of Kress's work, though, which I feel needs challenging if we are to establish more precisely the modal parameters within which creativity and learning occur. This feels slightly churlish given the wealth of ideas he has given the subject, many of which are incorporated here. However, his work insufficiently accounts for how the mind processes the material it receives, no matter in what form. For what exactly does Kress mean when he writes that "[t]he signs that are made by readers in their reading draw on *what there is to be read*"? Does this mean that when a student reads written text then a form of writing is remade in the mind? And that if he or she reads a film then a series of moving images replays in his or her head? This is a curious claim to make and also precludes the fact that people have been 'reading' the visual for centuries in what they see in front of their eyes. It is, of course, perfectly possible to envisage the mind as processing information metaphorically as images. Leading neuroscientist Antonio Damasio (2000) likens human consciousness to a "movie-in-the-brain" (9) although he qualifies this by saying "that in this rough metaphor the movie has as many sensory tracks as our nervous system has sensory portals – sight, sound, taste, and olfaction, touch, inner senses, and so on" (9). In his model consciousness comes before language, as demonstrated by the ability of some people with damage to the part of the brain that controls language to continue to have an awareness of self and others (108–112). But while it might well be a model in which "[m]ovies are the closest external representation of the prevailing storytelling that goes on in our minds" (188), it is not an argument for the visual to dominate learning. The 'movie-in-the-brain' is part of 'core-consciousness', that which gives us a *sense* of being human but which remains unarticulated. The verbal ruptures this 'core-consciousness', forcing the mind to make choices and generate meaning in ways more multiple than when reliant on other modes. Vygotsky (1986 [1936]) points the way to this when he writes that "[t]hought is not merely expressed in words; it comes into existence through them" (218). Thought can perhaps come into existence through the visual too. I can watch a film and then demonstrate my thoughts about it by making my own version, posting it on Youtube for the world to see. But I would question the degree to which this process can be categorised as thinking if no verbal intervention occurs. Such re-creation absolutely adds to the learning process, as argued for strongly in Chapter 5. However, it fails to account for the reflective nature of learning and the role the verbal plays, not just in representing the world, but in bringing thought into being. For what happens when my ideas about the film posted on Youtube change over time? How might these be expressed? Short of making yet another film I cannot present them visually. Yet I can do so verbally with ease. And I can do so in my head as well as in articulating changes to others by speaking or writing. To quote Kress back at him, we cannot endlessly rely on "showing the world". Only in "telling the world" – a process given prominence in the chapter on re-creativity – can we work on it effectively, intervene in radical fashion, explain our choices, check for understanding, point directly to further developments, track change over time and hand on knowledge in ways that are sophisticated yet relatively lacking in ambiguity. Only in recourse to the verbal can we move our consciousness beyond the endless replaying of a "movie-in-the-brain". This is not the conclusion of a speculative English practitioner, but of the neuroscientist quoted above: "Creativity itself – the ability to generate new ideas and artefacts – requires more than consciousness can ever provide. It requires abundant fact and skill memory, abundant working memory, fine reasoning ability, language" (Damasio 2000: 315). We live in exciting times. Any school that fails to allow young people to make films, produce radio broadcasts and build websites is letting them down. But the same goes for any school that neglects the importance of verbal modes within the multimodal landscape. Language – and I do feel it is a term that can account for the various forms that words take, even when discussing modality – holds the key to the "cognitive fluidity" (Mithen 1996) that is so crucial to successful learning. With this in mind, the examples that follow take every opportunity to focus on how using a range of modes in the classroom can not only increase learning in general, but how it can increase verbal capabilities. Several explicitly direct students to reflect on the possibilities and limitations of the verbal, as it interacts with other modes. This focus on language, within a chapter on modality, is offered as a way of re-invigorating the subject's traditional focus while embracing new developments. It is a way of re-positioning the verbal rather than pushing it aside. It is certainly not an attempt to hold on to English's linguistic base in a way that risks conferring on it the indignity of becoming "the 'Latin' or the 'Classics' of the present period" (Kress in Goodwyn 2004: 117).

Images and words

The creativity of words and images combine powerfully in picturebooks and graphic novels. These are useful forms to use in the classroom given the obvious connections between visual and verbal elements of the texts and the possibilities for sustained reflection offered by both in ways not available in moving image media.

I want to offer a model in which the creativity of images stimulates the creativity of words. In this model, images are placed in a position analogous to the cloud in Vygotsky's statement, "A thought may be compared to a cloud shedding a shower of words" (1986 [1936]: 25), used to illustrate the creativity existing in the interplay of thought and language. A thought, no matter how complex, can be reduced to a single whole, a unit of sense. For example, I can hold a single thought under the banner of 'creativity', which contains the ten chapters, the multiple sub-chapters and the seventy thousand or so words of this book. In order to articulate my thoughts about the book, I must shed a shower of words – indeed, I have done so and it is the physical object you have before you. Armstrong (2000: 140) calls this an act of translation and refers to the "linguistic creativity" by which it "attempts to seek a unique equivalent for unique inner speech". An image, like a thought, can be conceived of as a single unit. Multiple elements can be taken in at a glance and held in the mind as sense. But once that sense is acted on, once the viewer seeks to articulate what he or she sees, it can be translated into words. In such a case, the image, like the cloud, produces a shower of words.

It is this translation of images into words that I want to put forward as the process by which they can be most usefully 'read' in the English classroom. In drawing attention to the process, teachers can help students understand the capacity for 'linguistic creativity' that they possess over all texts: once they have experienced turning pictures into words (both through simple descriptive exercises, but also through placing meaning on pictures) they can do the same thing with other modes, turning music, or architecture, or fashion ranges into words. Just as significantly, they can turn one set of words into another, through *re*-creation or interpretation. To be clear: I am not arguing that various modes cannot stand alone as systems of meaning. Images or sounds do not have to be translated into words and to do so fundamentally alters their attempts at representation. However, a dialogic engagement with these modes sets in place cognitive processes that are then most readily articulated in words. And these words are important because they are the nearest we can get to what students actually think about things.

Reading images

The Arrival, by Shaun Tan (2007), is a novel composed entirely without words. The reader – though viewer might be more apt – constructs a narrative by making connections between a series of drawn images. What follows offers a staged approach to using the book to develop an understanding of the wider meaning of reading among secondary age students: in how reading images is an activity worthy of engagement in itself and also how it allows for reflection on reading words.

FIGURE 3.1 Image from Shaun Tan's *The Arrival* (2007)

Stage 1: reading the whole story in a single image

At the centre of *The Arrival* is the story of a father leaving his family behind to seek work in a foreign land. A single image (see Figure 3.1) offers a visual representation of the family's separation. Before looking at the rest of the story, or any aspects of the book's design, students should study this picture in small groups and make predictions about the whole narrative. 'Reading' the picture helps develop an awareness of how an image works on them and how they bring meaning to it. Creativity occurs in the interaction between what can be seen in the picture and what it leads viewers to think, as they connect it to their existing knowledge of images and of the world in general. This awareness can be heightened by asking students to respond to the following prompts in stages:

1. Give two different accounts of what is happening in this picture.
2. What is the relationship of the man to the figures in the suitcase? How do you know?
3. From looking at this picture, what do you think the story as a whole will be about?
4. What ideas come into your mind when considering the colour, style and general details of the picture?
5. What are the spiky marks in the back panel of the suitcase and why are they there?

The questions move from the general to the specific in order to match the process of reading an image. The eye takes in the picture as a whole and begins to form conclusions, before homing in on details and refining those details. Concluding the activity by directing students to discuss how reading this picture compares to reading words on a page enables reflection on the general process of extracting and generating meaning from any symbolic representation.

Stage 2: reading the whole book in a minute

While the cover and blurb of a written novel give significant clues as to what is about, flicking through the text for a minute is unlikely to reveal much more. This is not the case with a graphic novel. As we have seen, an image can be processed very quickly and provide its own narrative in microcosm. This process is magnified when a single glance takes in the multiple images that might be contained on a double-page. Moving back and forth between pages develops it further still. The following activity allows students to gain an impression of what *The Arrival* is about by quickly browsing through its pages before they engage in serious sequential reading. Each of the three tasks should be completed in a minute so that students can reflect on how effectively the eye can process a series of images in a short space of time.

1. Students skim-read the book with no specific instructions. They explain what they think it is about, and why.

2. Different sections of the class skim-read with a focus. For example, one group looks at use of shading, another tries to pinpoint the dominant style of drawing, another the variations in style and another the different sizes of the pictures. The task demonstrates how meaning is built up through combining a range of modes, even in a book that at first glance appears mono-modal.

3. Different sections of the class look for different features of the text. For example, one group looks for themes, another focuses on the central character, another on the setting and another the use of realism and surrealism. Again, the focus is on how meaning is built up through combining all the different elements of a text.

Stage 3: reading intertextuality

Tan's book is not completely wordless. A note at the back reveals that the story was inspired by his own father's arrival in Australia from Malaysia in the 1960s. It also lists visual references and inspirations that include picture postcards from New York at the start of the twentieth century, photographs of street scenes from post-war Europe and Gustav Doré's 1870 engraving, 'Over London by Rail'. For this task, students are shown examples of the source material and must then find pictures in the novel that they think were influenced by it. They should be given the opportunity to research details around the original in order to make suggestions as to how referencing the material adds meaning to the book. Thus they are not only exploring modality but also the creativity of intertextual referencing, which allows for the possibility of meaning being generated through suggested relationships with other texts (New London Group 1996). Students should also search through the whole book to find other pictures that remind them of images they have seen elsewhere.

Stage 4: reading the pictures in sequence

Narrative writing is governed by "the logic of time" (Kress 2003: 1) so that the reader must work through a text from beginning to end in order to gain a full understanding. That understanding relies on the "movingness" (Fish 1990: 44) of a written text, in which meaning evolves as one word builds on another. In contrast, the image is governed by "the logic of space" (Kress 2003: 2), which allows a reader to absorb its different elements in a single glance and to dwell on the particulars of those elements for as long or short a time as desired. A graphic novel, even one made entirely of images, is a hybrid of both logics. The reader must move through the images in time, but can stop and absorb any single image or flick back and forth at will. Perhaps the key difference in the temporal element of this process between written text and graphic text is in the smoothness of transition from one moment to the next. While reader-response theory explains that meaning is created as much through exploring the gaps in a text as what is actually written (Iser 1978; Fish 1990), there is still an impression of continuity of action, interrupted at relatively large intervals by text markers, such as blank spaces or new chapters. In graphic texts the reader is constantly aware of jumping from one moment to the next. Meaning is much more obviously generated in the ever-present gap between images, or the "gutter" as comic-book writers call it (McCloud 1994).

A task to encourage reflection about reading pictures asks students to construct their own theory as to how pictures are read and how it compares to reading writing. After an initial discussion groups should word explanations for the following:

- Develop a theory about how the reader knows what has happened in the "gutter" that separates images.
- Develop a theory about how the size of the panels creates different meanings.
- Develop a theory about how the use of close-ups, long-shots, etc. creates meaning.
- Develop a theory about how facial expressions create meaning in this book.
- Develop a theory about what this book would be like if it was written in words rather than pictures. Write the opening paragraph to such a book.

The task helps students understand the creativity of images, both as single entities and in sequence. It also helps them to reflect on how, as readers, they must bring meaning to a text and construct a narrative alongside that provided by the author.

Stage 5: re-creating the text

It is tempting to suggest a wordless approach to *The Arrival*. Students read it in silence without discussion. They are left with their own personal engagement with the book, their cognitive processing perhaps existing as some kind of visual sense, resisting transformation into words: a condition in harmony with a silent graphic novel. Such an approach might, however, reveal the limitations of the visual. For no matter the sophistication and ready availability of digital technologies, it is difficult, if not impossible, to engage in immediate, reflective, dialogic responses without words. We are back to the idea of images being analogous to Vygotsky's cloud that produces a shower of words: both image and cloud are filled with potential, which is released in the transformation from one mode to another. Consequently, if images are to have a significant impact on learning in English, teachers must consider the creativity of 'transduction', of moving from one mode to another, in this case from the image to the word. However, in order to stress that meaning can be multimodal, better still design an activity that draws on both the image and the word. One possibility is to ask students to create a documentary-style commentary for the father's journey and his eventual reunification with his family. Students select ten to twenty key images that cover the broad span of the narrative. They then write an outline of this narrative in the style of a documentary voiceover. In this instance they experience not only the transformation in meaning brought to a text by combining modes, but also that which occurs in transferring the text from one medium to another.

Combining words and still images in children's picturebooks

At first it seems counter-intuitive to use picturebooks written for very young children in the secondary classroom. However, these books have an underlying sophistication in the way they combine words and images sufficient to be explored in a range of academic works (Nodelman 1990; Lewis 2001; Arizpe and Styles 2003; Nikolajeva and Scott 2006; Evans 2009) along with an accessibility that makes them very useful for exploring the creativity generated by words, images and the multimodal interaction of the two. In particular the picturebook medium enables contemplation of the reading process itself in a way not so obviously present in other media: for as the eye moves from image to word and back again, readers can consciously consider how meaning is generated in both modes. They must balance the competing demands of words and images, particularly in texts that place them in ironic juxtaposition to one another so that they "challenge readers to make their own interpretations" (Arizpe and Styles 2003: 27).

Looking at the written text of a picturebook, without recourse to the pictures, provides a useful starting point for an exploration of the co-dependency that exists between words and images in generating meaning. Without both meaning is incomplete. The text of Eileen Browne's (1994) *Handa's Surprise*, printed in its entirety, shows this to be the case:

> Handa put seven delicious fruits in a basket for her friend, Akeyo. She will be surprised, thought Handa as she set off for Akeyo's village. I wonder which fruit she'll like best? Will she like the soft yellow banana . . . or the sweet-smelling guava? Will she like the round juicy orange . . . or the ripe red mango? Will she like the spiky-leaved pineapple . . . the creamy green avocado . . . or the tangy purple passion-fruit? Which fruit will Akeyo like best? "Hello, Akeyo," said Handa. "I've brought you a surprise." "Tangerines!" said Akeyo. "My favourite fruit." "TANGERINES?" said Handa. "That *is* a surprise!"

With no knowledge of the images, it is impossible to work out what is happening. Handa has placed seven fruits in a basket for Akeyo. Tangerines are not among them and yet when she meets her friend they seem to be the only fruit on show. Thus a class given this text becomes engaged in trying to work out possible reasons for the conclusion. There are no clues in the words, so any solution is purely specu-lative. However, the absence of images allows students to consider the function of the words beyond telling a story. Likely responses are that they are designed to teach young children about fruits, numbers, colours, hyphenating, alliteration, ellipsis, questioning, tense, use of speech and possibly more. The list is long, given the text's brevity. In addition the teacher can draw attention to possible inferences in the text, for example asking for ideas about the age of the girls, the nature of their relationship and the setting. More importantly, the class can be challenged to explain how they make these inferences. In concluding that they come from prior knowledge of how books for young children work and existing knowledge of the world, they are exposed to the idea that reading is something more than decoding the written word. In not being able to work out fully what is happening, they also see that writing relies on the author providing the reader with sufficient information for full understanding and that any text, whether it uses pictures or not, cannot realise its potential for meaning without being consumed in totality. The creativity of a text relies on it being complete; readers can only generate a satisfyingly coherent meaning for a text if it provides them with sufficient information.

When students read the pictures in *Handa's Surprise*, alongside the words, the full story is instantly clear (see Figure 3.2). As Handa walks along with her basket of seven fruits a different animal steals a different fruit on each page without Handa realising (though variations in her facial expressions and hand and arm movements show she knows that *something* is happening to the contents of the basket). Finally, a goat butts a tree, sending a shower of tangerines down into the empty basket.

FIGURE 3.2 Image from Eileen Browne's *Handa's Surprise* (1994)

But it is not just the storyline that can be read from the pictures. The setting is recognisably African, made apparent by the animals, the village setting, the girls' clothing and the way Handa walks with her basket on her head. This is confirmed in the book's imprint, which explains that it is set in a particular region of Kenya and that Handa is a member of the Luo tribe. All these points, and how they are perceived by readers, feed into an understanding of the story.

Boxes 3.1 to 3.3 outline further activities that show the generativity of words combined with images. All use picturebooks and can be put to good use in English classrooms seeking to develop creativity and learning.

BOX 3.1 Contemporary images with traditional narratives

Anthony Browne's (1981) *Hansel and Gretel* is a particularly interesting storybook to use for an exploration of how images and words combine. While the written text sticks to a traditional telling of the fairy story, complete with a woodcutter, an evil stepmother, a witch and a house made of bread and cake, the illustrations are recognisably modern. This is further complicated by the inclusion of traditional fairy story images, such as a witch's hat, within the modern pictures (see Figure 3.3). The effect is to

FIGURE 3.3 Image from Anthony Browne's *Hansel and Gretel* (1981)

have two separate stories operating simultaneously that fuse into one: the traditional tale of children having to grow up and find their own way in the world sits alongside a modern one addressing issues of poverty, dysfunctional family life and neglect. Activities based around the book can explore the darkness contained in the images that is not as obviously present in the writing. This allows for reflection on how and why (if at all) the images transform the meaning of the traditional tale.

BOX 3.2 The transition from still to moving images

Julia Donaldson and Axel Scheffler's (1999) *The Gruffalo* is a well-known and relatively straightforward picturebook recently made into an animated film. The film sticks closely to the book and makes no significant additions, yet it is about half an hour long, while the original only takes a few minutes to read. In a sense the significance of this adaptation lies in the change of medium rather than mode, from page to screen. However, it is useful to consider the different impact of the mode of the moving image compared to that of the still, particularly in asking whether one is easier to 'read' than the other. A fruitful approach is to ask students to generate their own ideas for adapting the picturebook before they watch the film. They can be encouraged to think about the different modes used in a film, specifically considering how to turn still images into moving ones and what sound to add. Focus in watching the film can be on techniques for expanding its length, including the inclusion of panning shots and a voiceover narrative.

BOX 3.3 Giving meaning to nonsense

Christopher Myers (2007) offers a version of *Jabberwocky* that uses the original text and yet, through the juxtaposition of images, presents it as a basketball game. An afterword gives some justification for the choice of subject matter, but essentially the book shows the creativity that can occur in filling nonsense words with meaning. Images in this case do not so much reflect, adapt or complement the meaning of the writing as bring it into being. The juxtaposition of particular nonsense words next to particular images give them, in that particular space, an actual meaning. Secondary students might find this text useful as a starting point for attaching an entirely different narrative to *Jabberwocky*, or for writing a nonsense poem of their own to which they can subsequently assign meaning. The exercise draws attention to how meaning needs to be situated in a context. Words cannot generate meaning if they have no context at all, be that related to a particular use or to all previous uses.

Exploring the mode of sound

If, as suggested in exploring the link between images and words in picturebooks, coherent meaning can only come in considering a text in its entirety, then importance must be given to the mode of sound whenever it occurs. The activity outlined in Box 3.4 suggests listening initially only to the sound in moving image media. This serves two main functions: first, it forces students to engage with a mode that is often overlooked and, second, it draws attention to how the creativity of a text relies on all its modes for completion. Sound adds meaning not present in other modes but on its own does not fully make sense.

BOX 3.4 Sound first: Building up to the creativity of the whole

The Oscar-winning animated short film adaptation of Shaun Tan's *The Lost Thing* (2010) has been selected for this activity in order once again to draw on the author's striking and unusual visual imagery. However, in this case, the images are initially ignored in order to focus on sound. This then builds up to an understanding of the whole film when approached in stages as outlined below:

1. Listen to the first minute of *The Lost Thing* with the screen turned off. Students jot down individually everything they hear. They are likely to make references to melodic, melancholic music, background traffic (probably a train or a tram), footsteps and a voice, which they might identify as Australian and will probably think is unhappy, or at least downbeat. His first words are, "So you wanna hear a story . . .." and the minute ends with him saying, "So maybe I'll just tell you about the time I found the lost thing . . .." At this stage don't ask for comments on what the story might be about, simply what is heard.

2. Listen to the sound of the first minute again. This time give separate groups a particular focus. One group should concentrate on the voice

---

of the narrator, another on the music and another on background noises. Take feedback from groups about what they hear. When this is done lead a discussion speculating on what the film is about. Encourage students to justify their thoughts in relation to their knowledge of how sound works in other films.

3. To expand initial thoughts on what the film is about, ask small groups to write the opening line to a short story based on what has been heard. Having listened to a selection, ask groups to complete a short opening paragraph. Rather than hearing these responses, ask groups to write a single sentence beginning "Our short story is about . . ..". This focus on the "aboutness" of texts (Reid in Dean and Barton 2011) is intended to move students on from worrying about unearthing what they mean, instead relying on an immediate, more visceral response, something that will be helpful when they view the rather abstract film as a whole.

4. Watch the first minute of *The Lost Thing*. Lead a discussion on how expectations have been met or confounded. Discuss how meaning has been changed by the introduction of images, and, in particular, by the animated format.

5. Watch a further five minutes. Ask small groups each to concentrate on different modes of meaning: for example, on colour, non-diagetic sound, diagetic sound, images. Discuss the impression created by each.

6. Watch the end of the film. Return to the idea of "aboutness". Each student writes a sentence beginning "This film is about . . .". Read a selection of responses and then ask for the sentence to be continued beginning with the words "and how . . ." (Reid in Dean and Barton 2011). In responding in this way, students are considering the creativity of the film as a whole: how it has affected them and their own particular response. Given that the film has a non-naturalistic setting, with many of its objects, including 'the lost thing', unidentifiable in everyday life, this helps reassure students that they can still talk in knowing terms about something even when it denies any obvious interpretation. Importance is given to what they can say about what they do know, rather than what they cannot say about what they do not know. For creativity works with the known, what is there, and where there are gaps it brings meaning into being.

Conclusion

When our mind receives information, it does not consciously reflect on the mode in which it comes. Nor, for most of the time, are we aware of processing this information. We may exist in a sensual world and while awake can never turn off our senses to that world, but we do not articulate how world and senses interact every moment of every day. For example, you are not – until I have put it in your mind just now – contemplating the feel and texture of your seat yet in some way your body and mind are aware of it. I make this point as a prelude to a final note on a key difference between verbal modes and others. We receive the world through our senses. These senses act on the mind consciously or otherwise. So, in most cases, we see, hear, feel, smell and taste as a matter of course. We also receive sensory information in multiples rather than isolated forms, so it would seem that we experience life itself in a multimodal way.

Language use does not work in the same way. While in our social world we do speak as a matter of course, our competence in using language has a profound impact on the way we engage with the world in general. The greater the sophistication and control we have over language, the greater our ability to think about, bring meaning to, and manipulate thinking about our existence. Of course, it can be argued that such sophistication applies to other modes. There is a grammar of visual design (Kress and Van Leeuwen 1995), for example, competence in which allows for the generation of particular forms of meaning. But at issue when thinking about learning is the part this mode plays in thought itself. We are back to Vygotsky's key point that we do not think in words but that words bring thought into being. They are the means of sorting out a response to the multimodal stimulation of life in general. The greater our capacity to use language, then, the greater our capacity to think: and this involves thinking about, using and interpreting other modes. Wolf (2008), in exploring the impact of reading on the brain, argues that "[c]hildren with a rich repertoire of words and their associations will experience any text or any conversation in ways that are substantively different from children who do not have the same stored words and concepts" (9). The text does not have to be a written one. Wolf makes the comment in speculating on how an increased capacity for language use leads to an increased ability to transform the material of our existence: in other words, the more competent we are at using language the more competent we are likely to be at drawing meaning from a full range of modes of communication. The remaining chapters in this book draw heavily on the learning and creativity that come from the transformation of texts. It is perhaps fitting to end here, then, with a quotation from Wolf (2008: 17–18) suggesting that all transformation rests ultimately in the ability of language to manipulate and conceive of various meanings, and that this capacity, in turn, is heightened by competence in being able to decode and bring meaning to words:

> the goal of reading is to go beyond the author's ideas to thoughts that are increasingly autonomous, transformative and ultimately independent of the

written text. From the child's first, halting attempts to decipher letters, the experience of reading is not so much an end in itself as it is our best vehicle to a transformed mind, and, literally and figuratively, to a changed brain.

Key texts

Cope, B. and Kalantzis, M. (eds) (2000) *Multiliteracies: Literacy learning and the design of social futures.* London: Routledge.

Kress, G. (2003) *Literacy in the New Media Age.* London: Routledge.

Kress, G. (2010) *Multimodality: A social semiotic approach to contemporary communication.* London: Routledge.

Creativity as re-creativity

... any speaker is himself a respondent to a greater or lesser degree. He is not, after all, the first speaker, the one who disturbs the eternal silence of the universe.

Mikhail Bakhtin, "The Problem of Speech Genres"

Sentences end with full-stops. Stories do not.

Harold Rosen, Stories and Meanings

Re-creativity, closely related to concepts of *transformation* (Knights and Thurgar-Dawson 2006) and *re-framing* (Andrews 2010), refers to the self-conscious manipulation of source material to bring something new into being. A process analogous to learning, its exploration is particularly pertinent here. For learning involves working on new material or on what is already known to bring advanced or new meaning and knowledge into being. The existing knowledge of students and the additional material to which they are introduced is *re*-created at the point at which learning occurs.

In a way, the term seems unnecessary. If we accept that creativity – and learning – does not occur in a vacuum, then it must draw on existing resources anyway. However, the *re-* prefix makes explicit the intention to work actively upon and *transform* specific material; it cultivates careful thought about source material and encourages a direct comparison between an original and what it inspires. Thus it demands reflexivity, requiring students to think carefully both about the impact of resources presented to them in lessons and what they do with them. It stresses the active nature of creativity, that it involves working on material to make it one's own, as meaning is simultaneously *transferred* into a new realm and *transformed* into a new shape. *Re-creativity* also encourages teachers to think carefully about classroom resources. Acknowledging the transformative nature of learning removes the temptation simply to hand knowledge on to students as a given, while also opening up possibilities for dialogic practice: with meaning being generated in multiple interactions between what teachers and students bring to classrooms and what teachers and students do with it.

It is worth making one caveat about re-creativity. It should not be applied indiscriminately to all classroom activities that work on resources. In theory, writing an academic essay about a novel is a form of re-creativity, taking the original and making it afresh as a critical inquiry into what it means. But to say as much is to belittle both essay writing and re-creativity. The former offers a critical engagement with a text while the latter seeks to mirror, in some way, the creative process that brought the original into being: it can cast critical light on a text (as explored further in Chapter 8) but that is not its primary purpose. Consequently teachers need to think carefully about how and why to make activities re-creative. For it is not a straightforward process; students may well find it hard to access material and so struggle to be re-creative. Teachers, though, might use this to their advantage. In identifying manageable but challenging re-creative tasks, even when students are struggling with understanding, they can help them to access material; and as understanding increases, so the quality of what is re-created improves. This two-way process encourages reflection on the subject matter of English, but also on learning itself.

New possibilities for re-creative work have emerged in recent years with the rapid development of new media technologies. Where once students could conceive of a film adaptation of a short story, now they can make one themselves; where once they could storyboard images to go with a poem, now they can bring the storyboard to life on a computer, adding in sound effects as they go. Re-creating material in an entirely different medium offers students some of the most exciting ways of working on material and is explored elsewhere in this book. This chapter offers a more traditional approach with a particular focus on writing and speaking as re-creative activities. Primarily this comes from a belief that re-creativity has its roots in simple acts of *re-telling*; if students are to transform material into any number of forms, both ones with which they are familiar and otherwise, then they must have the opportunity, initially, to handle that material in familiar ways. This means allowing them to relate material *in their own words*. This is not naively to suggest that students have a core language identity from which all meaning flows, but it is to accept that young people have a right to discuss and write about material without being self-conscious about the particular forms used. Once they have done this – made the material their own – then they can begin to explore different forms of manipulation, moving from *re-telling* to *re-creating*. While this has been common practice in many classrooms for years, it sits uncomfortably with a genre approach to English that stresses that all language use is a form of discourse and so denies the possibility of any speaker having his or her 'own voice'. Consequently the chapter draws upon work that pre-dates the genre approach, particularly Rosen's (1985, 1988) ideas about re-telling and the everyday uses of narrative and de Certeau's (1988) about "re-writing". In doing so, it makes its own suggestions about a *writer-response* approach to texts before moving on to explore ideas of *extreme re-creativity* in which the re-creative act itself is privileged over the content of work produced. All this is preceded by an attempt to develop a theory of re-creativity as it links to English.

Developing a theory of re-creativity

Several prominent theorists of creativity and related topics make it clear that all creativity is *re*-creativity. Any form of expression or communication, if it is to have intelligible meaning, must draw on what has gone before. Pope (2005) refers to re-creativity as "the ongoing process of making afresh" (84) and argues that it "turns upon the relation between what has happened so far and what may happen now and now and now (i.e. 'next' conceived as an unfolding series)"; Attridge (2004), writing about literature, comments that "[t]he creative act, however internal it might seem, works with materials absorbed from a culture or a *melange* of cultures" (36), while Kearney's (1988) study of the imagination in Western culture presents the postmodern age as one in which the idea of "the artist as one who not only emulates but actually replaces God" (12) is superseded by the idea of "the *bricoleur*: someone who plays around with fragments of meaning which he himself has not created".

Such a focus on creativity as an ongoing process stemming from what already exists, rather than as emerging from a divine source, or from the mind of an individual genius, is compatible with a constructivist view of learning as a process of meaning-making and building 'possible worlds' (Bruner 1986). Learning is socially constructed, guided by the particularities of an individual's social existence, so that any creativity with which he or she engages must be drawn from his or her wider environment. This does not mean that all stimulus material leads to the same response from those who receive it, but that a range of responses, within certain constraints, is always available. Learning involves understanding how to draw on these responses, adapt them, re-invent them and link them to prior knowledge and understanding.

Seeing re-creativity as dependent upon working with existing materials also gives teachers an important role in promoting conditions for learning. If young people are not provided with suitable resources then re-creativity is impossible. Re-creativity, like the imagination, does not lie solely within our heads, but in the stimulation brought to our thought processes by exposure to external stimulation. The richer and more suitable the material provided for working upon then the more imaginative or creative is that which can potentially be produced. If "[w]e can only construct possible worlds, can only think of things as possibly being so, out of what we already know" (Egan 1992: 52) then "the richness, variedness, unusualness and effectiveness of our imaginative activity will turn in significant degree on how much it has to compose or construct with" (53).

The idea that some resources are more open to imaginative transformation than others has implications for English teaching beyond the simple matter of stimulation. It also allows a case to be made for the validity of certain resources over others as carrying within them qualities that encourage transmission with variation, by embodying qualities of 'memetics' (Dawkins 1989 [1976]; Blackmore 1999), the term that identifies the cultural spread of material as analogous to genetic transmission. Certain cultural forms survive and adapt to new times and circumstances because of the multiple possibilities for meaning they make available. These resources, more than others, carry within them possibilities for moving thought and learning forward into new imaginative and creative territory.

'Memetics' challenges links between creativity and originality. If culture is passed on, albeit with variation, then it is not original. Attridge (2004) offers an alternative conceptualisation of this point, by drawing a clear distinction between creativity and originality. In his argument creativity bears a strong resemblance to what we are calling re-creativity, involving the re-working of available cultural materials; in contrast, originality requires the creation of "something that marks a significant departure from the norms of the cultural matrix within which it is produced and received" (35), resulting in a fundamental repositioning of the cultural field, knocking aside some old possibilities and putting new ones in place (36). Separating originality from creativity in this way bestows a democratic quality on both. For while originality results in material that is entirely unexpected and new, it immediately takes its place as part of a wider cultural matrix and so becomes available for others to work with, to *re*-create. We might not all be capable of originality, but we can all work with original material.

Reader-response theory (Iser 1978; Fish 1990) has a similarly democratising quality. In arguing that meaning comes not just from within a text but from responses to it, the theory gives control to readers, chipping away at a reverence towards canonical texts and allowing readers to value works of their own choosing. Reader-response might be seen as offering an initial step towards a full-blown theory of re-creativity. For in each new response offered, in the acknowledgement that within limits no two responses will be the same, new versions of a text emerge. They are new versions, however, in a very precise way. For the physicality of the text is not compromised in any way by reader-response. The words on the page remain the same. The transformation lies solely in the *reading* of the text. A theory of *re*-creativity moves beyond the fixed print (or image) physicality of the text, not so much chipping away at its reverential status as smashing it down. For once a text is re-created – given new shape and meaning by being re-written in any number of different ways – there is not even the possibility of it being read in the same way again. It is literally a different text, made afresh by what might be termed a *writer-response* approach.

Far from relegating reading to a lesser status, *writer-response* requires learners to read a text closely in order to have ideas about changing it. However, it is less intimidating for students because it lets them re-create according to their own wishes. They can even re-write so that something makes sense to them where the original does not. Even working within the liberating parameters of reader-response theory such freedom is not always possible, for students might not be confident in putting forward any response. Writer-response is not a magical solution in that some students will also be hesitant to re-write, but when it is done it gives a degree of authority to students that cannot come from reading alone. For once someone re-writes a text, it very much becomes his or her own.

Re-creativity, then, as a way of engaging with texts, differs from creativity in its conscious awareness not just that all creativity comes from somewhere, but that it comes from a particular place. It is a term that describes the process by which one text is deliberately transformed into another. Thus it involves much more focus on the making and production of texts than on their reception and consumption. It does not do away with ideas about creativity lying within texts studied in the classroom, but makes it clear that such creativity is worthless without the dialogic responses of learners. And in re-creative approaches they control the terms of those responses.

From re-telling to re-writing

Think about the last book you read. Now imagine re-telling the book to someone else. A simple enough process, but practical constraints relating to memory and time mean there is no possibility of the re-telling reproducing the exact words of the original. Instead any re-telling will offer a summary, selecting only the points it deems most pertinent. Decisions about what to include and exclude reveal a particular reading of the original. The re-telling is not just a re-telling; it is also a re-creation, an entirely new narrative, though one that would not be possible without an original.

Now think about the re-telling in relation to the original. What choices did you make? What does this suggest about your reading of the book? How might it differ from that of other people? What *re-creation* of the text have you brought into being? I ask these questions not because they are difficult, or because they are likely to result in profound advances in learning if and when they are offered to students; rather it is to highlight the complex patterns of meaning that can be established in the simplest of activities, activities with the potential to stimulate learning. In one sense there is only a limited value in encouraging students to summarise a book or a film in their own words: it might help them to remember plotlines or to write concisely. However, giving students responsibility for re-telling is a step towards acknowledging their right to take charge of their own learning, handing material over to them directly and laying the foundations for more challenging acts of re-writing.

The simple act of re-telling is also central to students being given a 'voice' in the classroom, in the sense not just that they are allowed to speak, but that they are guaranteed an audience and they can express themselves freely and without inhibi-tion. If they are denied this simple task how are they to be given opportunities to speak elsewhere? Rosen's (1985) work on "pupil-made narrative" (17) is driven by the frustrations he feels when confronted with the paradox that few areas of life limit opportunities for interaction – and so learning – as much as the classroom. Although his arguments are over two decades old, they still bear some pertinence. His point that "in most classrooms the chief and privileged story-teller (stories of any kind) is the teacher" (18) has subsequently been backed up by influential research-based studies (Wells 1986; Mercer 1995; Alexander, R. 2008). These call for a more dialogic approach to teaching and learning but in practice the situations Rosen recounts often remain all too familiar. At the most basic level they manifest themselves in the anxiety many teachers show in trying to ensure that students have a firm grasp of *what* is studied. With class novels and drama texts in particular, knowledge of basic plotlines is regularly reinforced, often through sorting activities that require students to place the most salient points of a plot in the correct order. I would challenge this practice. If your knowledge of *Macbeth*'s storyline is insecure, how much is it really improved by ordering a sequence of ten events? And why should those ten be accepted as the most important over another list? Students need to grapple with their own knowledge, no matter if it is limited, and develop it in conjunction with classmates. They need to dictate the *what*, not teachers. Teachers need only fill in any gaps as and when necessary. Box 4.1 outlines possible ways of structuring re-telling activities that require students to draw on what they themselves know and, in the process, re-create texts in some way.

BOX 4.1 Re-telling creatively

1. Building on key words:

■ The teacher writes ten key words relating to a story on the board. In pairs, students write a summary exactly a hundred words long containing all ten.

■ Pairs reduce the summary to fifty words. They try to keep as many of the key words as possible.

■ Pairs reduce the summary to a single sentence of no more than twenty words. They must use at least two of the key words.

2. Comparing key moments:

■ Pairs select what they consider to be the five key moments from a text.

■ They join up with another pair and compare key moments then negotiate to come up with a revised list of five.

■ Each group of four reads out its key moments to the whole class. A teacher-led class discussion produces a new list of five that meets with a general consensus. The teacher can intervene if he or she feels key moments have not been discussed.

3. Just a minute:

Pairs time each other to see if they can keep talking about the novel or play just read for a whole minute. Each student has a turn. After listening to one another, they construct a list of five to ten key moments from ideas that arose in their monologues.

As well as helping students to organise *what* is learned, re-telling also removes some of the anxiety they might have about *how* to respond to texts. This became clear to me in observing the difficulties trainee teachers sometimes have in helping students access even the most basic material, material which is perfectly suitable but somehow produces limited responses. One example involved teaching the conventions of book covers to Year 8. Heeding advice to access the students' prior knowledge, the trainee selected the cover from the first *Harry Potter* novel for analysis because most of the class would recognise it. She asked her students to annotate a photocopy, noting what they could see and what it might mean. She was surprised that the students were unable to move beyond simple denotations. For example, they would draw an arrow to the train in the centre of the picture and simply label it *train*, or to an area coloured red and label it *red*. When looking at lettering they struggled to comment beyond its size and position. In discussing the lesson afterwards we were both convinced that the students, though relatively low attaining, must have more to say about such a famous cover than that it is mainly red and has a train on it. They were struggling with the task because there was a mismatch between what they could potentially say about the cover and their inability to say this in the way specified by the task. They needed the opportunity to tell the story of the front cover in their own words (see Box 4.2). In describing what is going on in the picture, they can avoid the anxieties many students feel when asked to interpret a text or say what it *means*. They are engaging with the story actively springing from the cover rather than with what is hidden within.

BOX 4.2 Telling the story of a book cover

Stage 1: Re-telling

Rather than ask students to identify individual features, direct them to re-tell the story of the *whole* front cover. They might not initially know what an image or colour signifies, but they can explain what is happening in the overall picture. Stage this process using the following questions in pairs or small groups:

- In fifty to a hundred words describe what is happening in the picture.
- From the cover what can readers expect the story to be about?
- Pick three things about the cover that you think will be important to the story, e.g. an image, a colour, a style of font. Why do you think they will be important?

Stage 2: Re-creating

Re-creating the cover moves students one step closer to being able to engage critically with the original. Articulating their own design choices prepares them for analysing the initial model. If there is no time to design a new cover, then students can think about particular re-creative possibilities using a 'what if' framework:

- What if you change the colours of the cover?
- What if an image in the background is moved to the front of the picture?
- What if the author's name is in much bigger font?
- What if other characters are put on the cover?
- What if a photograph rather than an illustration is used for the cover?

Re-telling is only the start to further learning. For example, it remains the task of English teachers who encourage students to tell the 'story' of a book cover subsequently to guide them towards developing a discourse of critical analysis. But if teachers simply model how to do this without allowing students the opportunity to develop material in their own vernacular as a stepping-stone towards further learning, then students are unlikely to have sufficient material to offer up for analysis in the first place. Re-telling is part of the process by which learners can "go back and forth across the bridge from 'everyday discourse' into 'educated discourse'" (Mercer 1995: 83). It re-creates material on their own terms before teachers intercede to help "develop ways of talking, writing and thinking which will enable them to travel on wider intellectual journeys, understanding and being understood by other members of wider communities of educational discourse" (83).

Re-telling is no more than a basic form of re-creativity because, certainly at the point of arrangement, it lacks an *awareness* of how material is being re-shaped. *Re-creativity* demands a more conscious transformation of source material with choices made about form and content; it is also a further stage along in giving students control of their learning. The transformation is not just in the physical shape of the original text but also in its relationship to the learner. De Certeau (1988) outlines how until the end of the nineteenth century villagers in parts of rural France – particularly girls – were taught "just reading" (168), without recourse to writing. In other words, they were taught how to decode texts to the extent that they could follow script, but they were denied the opportunity to write themselves. This separation of reading and writing fosters a particular kind of passivity when faced with the written word: its authority quells oral questioning and the inability to write makes any kind of response impossible. It is a model in which "to write is to produce the text" while "to read is to receive it from someone else without remaking it" (169). Active reading approaches (Iser 1978; Fish 1990) go a long way to making sure that reading is not simply a matter of passive consumption; however, while a text remains only read, it is still at a distance from the actual experience of the learner. The text is there to act on the reader, even if the reader can decide the terms under which this occurs. It remains a text that has been produced and is being consumed *in a particular way*. When a text is re-written it is absorbed into the experience of the reader. The text is not so much something to learn *from* as to learn *with*. In effect, reading becomes an activity from which to draw resources for writing; reading provides material for "poaching" (de Certeau 1988: 165) and for re-using in the reader's own terms in what might usefully be termed a *writer-response*.

A writer-response has important consequences for the learning that can take place in relation to literary texts in particular. Literary texts are useful for demonstrating to students ways of using narrative to structure and bring meaning into existence. Their impact is limited, however, if they are seen as templates rather than as stimuli for such an ordering of experience. As templates they risk privileging particular approaches to using language in ways that may intimidate and even silence students. As stimuli they invite readers to re-write them, to make them relevant to their lives in whatever form they deem suitable. To this end the voice of the student should be privileged over the voice of the text, something that cannot happen if the text stands as an immutable object. Rosen (1988) calls for a "reworking of narratives" (22) that values the lives and stories of young people so that classrooms do not use literary texts to demonstrate how existence should be structured, but to give them the opportunity to create that structure themselves, be it as a reflection of their own selves or of a world of their imagining. Literary texts thus foster understanding and learning in the ways they enable "students to refashion them to their own meanings, influenced by the mobile and diversified culture which they are both living through and making" (22).

Writer-response: an alternative form of reading

A great truism of English Literature is that there are no wrong answers. Clearly this is not the case. While readers are free to place a range of responses upon a text, the text itself will be structured in such a way as to encourage particular responses. The reader is at liberty to wander far and wide from any intentions the author might have had, but stray too far and at some point the connection between the original text and meaning is lost. Contrary to popular belief, such thinking lies at the heart of reader-response theory (Iser 1978; Fish 1990).

Writer-response, however, is one instance in which the truism perhaps holds firm. When a student responds to a text by creating one of his or her own, notions of right and wrong tend to lose their relevance. There will be a dialogue taking place between the original and the new piece, but the burden of interpretation shifts. The student now has his or her own piece of work with no anxiety about what it means: with a direct personal connection to the work there is no need for the mediating process of meaning-making. The new text just is.

It is perhaps best, however, to regard this absence of right and wrong as a temporary situation, a starting point to a non-traditional form of critical textual exploration, one in which writing is a form of reading. *Re*-creativity cannot take place without an initial reading. Tellingly one of the few full-length studies of *re*-creative writing, or *transformative writing*, as it is called in the book, refers to reading ahead of writing in its title. *Active Reading: Transformative writing in literary studies* (Knights and Thurgar-Dawson 2006) explores how the study of literature at tertiary level can make use of a re-creative approach, placing importance on how writing derived from a source text reveals how that text has been read and is re-read in the re-writing. The active reader's motivation for writing does not lie, as it does with a 'creative writer' in "the creation of an autonomous and self-sustaining artistic product" (104) but in producing "a transformation in their understanding of the text with which they started".

Re-creativity and possible worlds

So far this chapter has focused on how re-creativity helps students to take control of learning, re-fashioning texts in keeping with their own worlds and world-views. Those world-views themselves, of course, exist within particular contexts. Thus I might well re-write a well-known story in my own words without consciously reflecting on choices of form and content, but choices will, nonetheless, be made. And they will, in turn, reflect in some way on the particular context of my own overall existence as well as the context within which the re-writing takes place. Using re-creativity like this offers a way into further learning, though perhaps advances learning itself only in limited ways. Learning can be advanced more fully when students are given opportunities to transform language consciously in multiple forms (see Box 4.3).

Writing something afresh in keeping with particular generic conventions, or with a focus on particularities of character, setting or plot, makes explicit "the way words actively articulate possible worlds rather than simply refer to a world that already exists" (Pope 2005: 85). It encourages students to take control of texts, not simply in the sense that they have ownership once something is in their own words, but because they are consciously dictating the linguistic terms within which re-creativity takes place. Consequently the re-creation is not just for themselves, but is directed towards a particular audience for particular purposes: it becomes situated in an actual context. Re-creativity with such a focus serves at least four learning functions: it offers a critical comment on the original text in the linguistic choices consciously made in the re-creation; it draws attention to the meaning that can be created from particular word and grammar choices; it develops writing within certain conventions; and it opens the mind up to new possibilities. Once re-creativity has occurred, material is brought into being for further transformation in an ongoing process of cognitive stimulation and re-stimulation. This latter point

---

BOX 4.3 Multiple ways to *transform* a text

The following list, by no means exhaustive, offers different ways to re-create a text. Each throws light on the original, while generating additional meaning. Students need to be practised in writing in these different forms, while the very process of doing so will advance their understanding of source material.

- writing a text in a different genre;
- writing a text in a different person;
- writing from the perspective of a different character;
- inserting yourself into a story;
- setting a text in a different time;
- setting a text in a different location;
- re-writing a text from memory alone;
- re-writing the beginning or ending of a text;
- writing a response to a character within a text;
- writing a 'gap' in the original text;
- using non-fictional forms to represent fiction (and vice versa).

---

sounds rather a grand claim to make about the simple act of writing something in a new way. This is not the intention. The transformation of a single text is unlikely ever to lead to a significant transformation of the way the world is understood and – contrary to what the current inspection regime in England seems to demand – it is pointless as English teachers for us to claim that huge leaps in learning can routinely occur within a single task; but we can stake a claim for the cumulative impact of strategies that work on and transform the materiality of the world. For in bringing a new world into being, students alter their own position within it, if only in fractional terms. Boxes 4.4 to 4.6 outline some activities in which this might occur.

BOX 4.4 Writing modern-day fairy stories

This re-creative activity was popularised through widespread use over many years of *Changing Stories* (Mellor, Hemming and Leggett 1984), a textbook for younger secondary students. It guides students in re-creating well-known fairy tales and also gives examples of re-creations, such as five versions of *Little Red Riding Hood*. By focusing on stories that have been passed down through many generations, students gain a sense of the different purposes to which stories can be set and of how meaning constantly changes according to the context in which they are told. Jack Zipes (2006) speculates on how fairy tales are a highly adaptive literary form with particular qualities that allow them to evolve and survive over hundreds of years; in other words, they are a form all about exploring and extending possible worlds. Older students might be interested in Zipes's ideas, particularly in relation to well-known modern versions of fairy tales, such as those in Angela Carter's *The Bloody Chamber* (1981). Younger ones might also consider how fairy tales adapt themselves to the modern world in exploring two recent re-creations of the Goldilocks story, Lauren Child's (2008) *Goldilocks and the Three Bears* and Anthony Browne's (2011) *Me and You*. Both bring new meaning to the story in the startling juxtaposition of a traditional tale with jarring images. Child uses a sinister-looking doll to represent Goldilocks and Browne's book runs illustrations showing the story of a young girl in a modern setting, who is separated from her mother, alongside illustrations more obviously relating to the fairy story.

BOX 4.5 Transforming fiction

In a sense writing an essay about a fictional text is a form of re-creation. The text is given new form in the shape of criticism. However, essay writing does not give the reader the kind of ownership enabled by transformative writing. The following are examples of how novels can be transformed into alternative texts:

- *Turning a novel into a board-game*: young readers respond well to making a board-game from a novel. The activity reinforces understanding of plot and also highlights some of the more ingenious devices used by an author to drive the narrative forward, as well as encouraging a focus on character and setting. This works particularly well for popular generic fiction that is increasingly used in secondary classrooms, such as Anthony Horowitz's *Alex Rider* series, Robert

Muchamore's *Cherub* books, Charlie Higson's *Young Bond* novels and Suzanne Collins's *Hunger Games* trilogy.

■ *Writing a report from a novel*: fictional characters often have qualities readily translated into psychological reports or profiles. Good examples include Shelter, the serial killer in Robert Swindells' *Stone Cold* (1993), and JJ, the child-killer in Ann Cassidy's (2005) *Looking for JJ*. Incidents in novels or short stories easily lend themselves to re-creation as newspaper reports. The murder of Sam the Onion Man in Louis Sachar's (2000) *Holes* is one example.

■ *Addressing a character as if he or she is real*: this activity can result in students engaging with large chunks of the source text, exploring it as fully as if they were to write a conventional essay. They focus on a theme or key incident in the text and in response write a letter to the main character involved. For example, students can write a letter to Christopher, the narrator of *The Curious Incident of the Dog in the Night-time* (Haddon 2005) explaining their thoughts on how he has told his story.

BOX 4.6 Playing with genre

The self-conscious demands genre writing places on language use provide lots of opportunities for re-creativity. The following are examples:

■ *Switching genre*: because of the way genre fiction tends to assign male and female characters to particular roles, re-writing that switches genders produces interesting effects. Re-writing a passage from James Bond so that the central protagonist is female is a good example.

■ *Re-writing newspaper reports as genre fiction*: the transformation from newspaper text to genre fiction reveals the tight, but very different constraints on which both types of writing rely.

■ *Genre and incongruity*: particular effect can be gained in writing one genre in the style of another. For example, a romance can be written in the style of science-fiction. The task is tricky but reveals the lexical fields and grammatical structures required by a particular genre and the difficulties in transferring one to another. A particularly good example to use with older students is the short story, 'Everything Ravaged, Everything Burned' (Tower 2009), a Viking saga written in the style of hard-boiled crime noir.

Extreme re-creativity

A genre-based approach to English is entirely compatible with a focus on creativity and linguistic experimentation. Its more sophisticated incarnations advocate manipulating and playing with genres – re-creating them – for particular effect as part of the process of becoming competent and adaptable in language use (Cope and Kalantzis 1993; Kress 1993). However, too rigid an application of the approach, a charge that can be levied in England at the *National Literacy Strategy*'s (DfES 2002) promotion of teaching writing through 'text-types' is open to criticism on two broad fronts (Robinson and Ellis 2000; Grainger, Gooch and Lambirth 2005). First, it requires students to use particular language conventions without having the opportunity to explore the process of text construction (Robinson and Ellis 2000) and, second, it denies the fluidity and flexibility existing in most written forms, regardless of their particular function. For example, there are several ways to write a persuasive text, many of which may incorporate other supposedly distinct text-types, yet the National Strategy outlines particular features of each identified text type that students must learn to replicate. The second criticism is particularly pertinent when considering creativity and learning. For there is a danger that an over-reliance on a text-type approach denies students the experience of writing as "a recursive, cognitive process" (73). Excessive focus on rules when writing limits the creativity that comes in the interplay between thought and writing. Writing no longer draws on thought for stimulation, but on a set bank of things to do.

Such a criticism is not to abnegate responsibility for teaching particular conventions of writing. All writing must conform to certain rules in order to make sense and communicate to an audience. Working within set forms can provide a "constraint satisfaction" in which "constraints should not be seen as restrictions on writing, but as means of focusing the writer's attention and channelling mental resources" (Sharples 1999: 6). The satisfaction comes from being able to write creatively within the constraints. In other words, they do not dictate precisely how one should write, but nor can they be ignored; the skilled writer modifies constraints for effect and in doing so reveals an awareness of how they work in the first place.

I would argue that there are only so many times a developing writer needs exposure to the rigid constraints of, say, instructional writing. Given that the features of such writing are taught explicitly to young people in England from Key Stage One all the way through to Key Stage Four, it is difficult to imagine the tedium induced when yet again being exposed to, say, a recipe and told to replicate its use of simple sentences, chronological connectives and command words. It seems reasonable, given the repetitive nature of much text-type work, to assume that more able students are bored with it by the time they reach secondary school and that less able students need a different approach if they have not achieved sufficient competence despite extensive exposure. One alternative is to guide students to become skilled writers within constraints in general rather than writing within the constraints of a particular text-type. In an approach that I would like to call *extreme re-creativity*, students work within very rigid, often very unusual bounds to help them learn to think carefully about how meaning is created and transformed. This, in turn, might help them think critically about their future use of more conventionally constrained writing.

Many of the ideas for *extreme re-creativity* are drawn from the *Oulipo* school of literature (Mathews and Brotchie 2005). *Oulipo* stands for *Ouvoir de Littérature Potentielle*, roughly translated as "workshop of potential literature". Founded by French writer Raymond Queneau in 1960 as a reaction to the unlimited freedom of Surrealism and still active today, "[t]he aim of the Oulipo is to invent (or reinvent) restrictions of a formal nature (*contraintes*)" (38–39). The movement does not see creativity and constraint as opposing forces, but as dependent upon one another. Thus "creation" is placed on the agenda of each monthly meeting of the group, in reference to "the presentation and discussion of new constraints" (39). The following examples show that the experimental writing practised by Oulipo draws attention to the crafted nature of creativity in writing; that writers have to work hard to create particular effects and that meaning is heavily influenced by the context within which something is written. *Extreme re-creativity* is a playful form of writing that encourages students to generate meaning within tight constraints.

Queneau's (2009) *Exercises in Style* re-creates a single, simple narrative ninety-nine times (see Box 4.7). In doing so it shows the effect different narrative choices can have on readers, but also the range of options open to a writer at the point of creation. The constraint here is the story rather than the form; placing the same story in multiple forms produces *multiple writings*. Interestingly Queneau rarely draws on established generic forms. His constraints are self-imposed, revealing new forms of creativity that can emerge from experimentation. Students can be encouraged to write their own experimental re-creations of a straightforward narrative using their own titles or borrowing from Queneau's own, which include *blurb*, *onomatopoeia*, *reported speech*, *official letter*, *rainbow*, *exclamations*, *comedy*, *feminine*, and *botanical*.

BOX 4.7 Multiple writings

Below are three examples from Queneau's *Exercises in Style*. The first is the template for the ninety-nine versions that follow in the full book.

Notation

On the S bus, in the rush hour. A chap of about twenty-six, soft hat with a cord instead of a ribbon, neck too long, as if someone's been tugging at it. People getting off. The chap in question gets annoyed with one of the men standing next to him. He accuses him of jostling him every time anyone goes past. A snivelling tone which is meant to be aggressive. When he sees a vacant seat he throws himself onto it.

Two hours later, I come across him in the Cour de Rome, in front of the Gare Saint-Lazare. He's with a friend who's saying: "You ought to get an extra button put on your overcoat." He shows him where (at the lapels) and why. (3)

Precision

In a bus of the S line, 10 m long, 3 wide, 6 high, at 3.6 km from its starting point, loaded with 48 people, at 12.17 p.m., a person of the masculine sex aged 27 years, 3 months and 8 days, 1.72 m tall, weighing 65 kg and wearing a hat 35 cm in height, round the crown of which was a ribbon 60 cm long, addressed a man aged 48 years, 4 months and 3 days, 1.68 cm tall and weighing 77 kg, by means of the 14 words whose enunciation lasted 5 seconds and which alluded to some involuntary displacements of 15 to 20 mm. Then he went and sat down about 1.1 m away.

57 minutes later he was 10 metres away from the suburban entrance to the Gare Saint-Lazare and was walking up and down over a distance of 30 m with a friend aged 28, 1.7 m tall and weighing 71 kg, who advised him in 15 words to move a button, 3 cm in diameter, by 5 cm in the direction of the zenith. (15)

Zoological

In the dog days, while I was in a bird cage at feeding time, I noticed a young puppy with a neck like a giraffe who, ugly and venomous as a toad, wore yet a precious beaver upon his head. This queer fish obviously had a bee in his bonnet and was quite bats, he started yak-yakking at a wolf in sheep's clothing claiming that he was treading on his dogs with his beetle-crushers. But the cock got a flea in his ear; that foxed him, and quiet as a mouse he ran like a hare for a perch.

I saw him again in front of the zoo with a young buck who was telling him to bear in mind a certain drill about his pelage. (107)

Re-writing can be more difficult with poetry, but if managed successfully enables students to engage with challenging material. Both examples in Box 4.8 are designed to remove anxiety students might feel in approaching poetry. The first requires them to re-create work in a shorter, more familiar form, thus encouraging a focus on core meaning; the second makes rather arbitrary changes, lending a playfulness to textual work and fostering imaginative critical responses that, given the absurdity of some of the language constructions produced, can be made without fear of making errors.

BOX 4.8 Re-creating poems

Re-writing poems as haikus

Students work on transforming whole verses into haikus, three line poems in a 5–7–5 syllable pattern. The process of reduction focuses attention on the essential meaning of a verse or passage.

Noun + 7

Students replace each noun in a poem with the seventh following it in a dictionary. Proper nouns remain the same. This results in very strange poems that lack obvious or coherent meaning. However, attention is focused on how new meaning is generated by the changes and on how important other word classes are in driving a poem forward. It also helps in reflecting back on the meaning of the original as in this version of the first verse of Wordsworth's "Daffodils". To maintain some semblance of rhyme and rhythm this version skips beyond the seventh noun on occasion to find a more suitable alternative:

> I wandered lonely as a clown
> That floats on high o'er vials and hulls
> When all at once I saw a crown,
> A hotbed, of golden Dormobiles
> Beside the lamb, beneath the tremors,
> Fluttering and dancing in the bruise.

Extreme re-creativity can appear excessively arbitrary. However, it places a very high demand on thinking carefully about word choices. Even in cases where the outcome is not strictly determined by the writer, such as the N + 7 activity, the absurdity and incongruity of many of the transformations still require the reader to work hard to bring meaning to the text. Arbitrary as it might seem, it requires precision and careful thought about how language is used. It might even be considered a parodic form of genre-writing, requiring linguistic tricks and ingenuity way beyond that of everyday language practices (see Box 4.9).

BOX 4.9 Extremely extreme re-creativity

Lipogram

This is a text that excludes a letter from the alphabet. The most famous example is George Perec's *La Disparation*, a detective novel written without an 'e' and, remarkably, translated as *A Void* (1994), by Gilbert Adair, using the same constraint. The translation is fifty pages longer than the original. The task takes a great deal of care and effort, forcing writers to focus on word choice and grammatical structure so as to maintain meaning. It works well in the classroom when asking students to translate a short passage of prose without using a particular letter, throwing light on the original word choices and their particular connotations. Here, for example, is the opening chapter to *Great Expectations*, then my attempt to write it without the letter 'e':

> My father's family name being Pirrip, and my Christian name Philip, my infant tongue could make of both names nothing longer or more explicit than Pip. So I called myself Pip, and came to be called Pip.

> My dad's family sign was Pirrip, and my Christian Philip, my infant talk could only say Pip. So I was Pip, and am Pip to this day.

Two points come to attention doing this task. The first is the degree to which Dickens's work depends on rhythm for its effect; the second is how much the letter 'i' occurs even in the original paragraph, giving it a visual as well as aural flow.

The prisoner's restriction

More able students may respond well to highly artificial and challenging restrictions such as this one. The writer must imagine he or she is a prisoner with a limited supply of paper and ink. To save resources writing must avoid letters that extend above or below the line, as in the following example:

> a russian con's economic missive
>   we were once seven con men, we are now seven cons. as communism was over we saw easier success in american consumerism, i.e. crime. in a moscow inn, we swore: seven is one, so one is seven . . . soon we came across a scam. our main man wove us a nice wee earner:–we own a zinc mine.

> (Ian Monk in Mathews and Brotchie 2005: 215)

Going for the limit

This involves seeing how far an original text can be reduced while maintaining some meaning. For example can a poem be reduced to a single word? *Daffodils*? Oulipo practitioners have even argued for the reduction of poems to single letters.

Several other books written in highly stylised form might also be of use in the classroom. *Eunoia* (Bok 2008) restricts itself to using one vowel only in each chapter, a different one each time. *The Interrogative Mood* (Powell 2010) is a novel written entirely in questions and Matt Madden (2006) pays homage to Queneau in re-creating a single comic page template in ninety-nine different ways. *Cloud Atlas*, by David Mitchell (2004), links a series of stories written in different genres and time periods. Each story ends halfway through before a central story is told to completion and the others start again, giving the text a deliberate pyramid structure. *If on a Winter's Night a Traveller*, by Italo Calvino (1982), a prominent member of Oulipo, is a complete novel paradoxically made up of a series of unfinished first chapters written in a range of styles. Geoff Ryman's (1998) *253* contains 253 character portraits, each 253 words long and about someone on an underground train of 253 seats, hurtling to its doom. And Dan Rhodes (2010) has written a collection of very short stories, each about one hundred words long. Highly stylised constraints on form are not limited to fiction either. For example, the Twitter social network site restricts the length of messages sent to a maximum of one hundred and fifty characters. Lengthy texts can be reduced to a single, or a series of, Twitter messages.

Extreme re-creativity is diametrically opposed to a functional approach to language learning. There is no social use in writing without using a particular letter, or in turning a poem into a single word. However, as well as giving students practice in crafting language to specific forms, it enables reflection on the writing process, on the generative capacity of language and on the fact that all language use is bound by particular constraints.

Conclusion

This chapter has tried to position re-creativity as a very specific practice, one that involves working directly on source texts in order to produce particular effects. In focusing initially on re-telling the intention was to suggest that re-creativity, like creativity, is an everyday human practice, part of the ordinary process by which we make sense of our world. Once we can tell the world in our own words we are in a position to learn more about it. Limiting opportunities for re-telling consequently limits opportunities for learning.

Re-creativity moves re-telling on so that students become conscious of the reasons for working on source material and can articulate transformative choices they have made. It allows for reflection both on the possible meanings of original material and what comes after. The focus here has been on the transformation of language, but teachers should also be aware of the learning opportunities opened up by transforming one mode into another. There is, indeed, an argument that such shifts are likely to offer more scope for learning than those that remain solely within the mode of written language. They encourage the mind's capacity for 'cognitive fluidity' (Mithen 1996) and stimulate a kind of *synaesthesia* of response, whereby meaning in one mode is accessed through another (Kress 2010; Ramachandran 2011), not just opening up a range of possible worlds, but a range of representations of those worlds.

The focus on the written word, however, is in keeping with a belief in the centrality of language in English and of the importance the ability to adapt and transform language has for learning. In becoming skilled in language use in all manner of contexts and forms – in being able to re-create language as and when necessary – young people can begin to take some control over the complexity of their lives. Re-creativity ensures that textual study in the classroom is not separate from those lives but can become an integral part of them. Texts are not there simply to tell us things or to be analysed, but are there to be worked upon, devices to help expand our world and our ability to transform the world. *Extreme re-creativity* takes this a stage beyond the everyday use of language, demonstrating its capacity for invention. Its possible worlds are verging on the impossible, reminding us of the paradox that while the word is capable of infinite variety, its most effective use always lies within socially constructed limits.

Key texts

Andrews, R. (2010) *Re-framing literacy*. London and New York: Routledge.
Knights, B. and Thurgar-Dawson, C. (2006) *Active reading*. London and New York: Continuum.
Mathews, H. and Brotchie, A. (2005) *Oulipo compendium*. London: Atlas Press.
Pope, R. (2005) *Creativity: Theory, history, practice*. London and New York: Routledge.
Rosen, H. (1985) *Stories and meanings*. Sheffield: NATE.

5

Creativity and the class novel

How does an entity or an idea unthinkable or unimaginable within existing frameworks of understanding and feeling come into being as part of our understood and felt world?

Derek Attridge, *The Singularity of Literature*

Resisting the pervasive sense of social paralysis, the poetic imagination would nourish the conviction that things *can be changed*. The first and most effective step in this direction is to begin to imagine the world as it is could be *otherwise*.

Richard Kearney, *The Wake of the Imagination*

Some years ago, after I taught a novel called *Bad Influence* (2004) to a Year 9 class, the author, William Sutcliffe, accepted an invitation to talk to my students. The occasion threw light on the different ways young people and adults experience reading. For what the students wanted to ask about above all else was the book's ambiguous ending, in which the exact details of a macabre crime committed by two young boys are withheld from the reader. To an adult such a conclusion serves an obvious function: it denies us the vicarious satisfaction of reading about a gruesome event – and forces us instead to think of the likely fate of the boys involved (we know they are arrested and tried, though we do not know exactly what for). When the author explained, however, that even he did not know exactly what happened, the students were infuriated. How could he not know the ending to his own book? In some ways, such a response is understandable in an age group with relatively limited knowledge of literature, indicative perhaps of a lack of exposure to texts that subvert readers' expectations. However, it also suggests that literature has a different effect on people depending on their stage of development. To an adult the ending of *Bad Influence* might be considered as opening up possibilities for creativity: the reader is left to fill in the gaps by bringing his or her own meaning to the conclusion. To a younger reader it is not so much creative as an artistic cop-out, leaving the reader starved of satisfaction. All this suggests that adults are prepared to place their own meaning upon texts, while younger readers expect texts to bring meaning to them.

Attempts at categorising reading habits according to age give some insight into the different interests of different groups. Thus, the 'reader as hero' from the ages of nine to thirteen (Appleyard 1994) seeks to identify with a central protagonist in order to experience the world through his or her eyes, with little desire for moral ambiguity or complexity. The 'reader as thinker' from the ages of fourteen to seventeen looks for books that stimulate thought but still resists actively imposing meaning on them, looking instead for one hidden meaning to be revealed. Such passive reception of reading material is problematic for creativity, seemingly denying an active, child-centred, enquiring approach. However, this chapter hopes to offer approaches that confront such apparent submissiveness. Young people might well, according to age, want to inhabit the role of hero or be told what a novel *really* means, but teachers can challenge this by developing activities that encourage the exploration of a whole variety of roles and that offer a wide range of interpretations. These activities force students to *do* things with texts, but they also draw attention to what texts can potentially *do* to young readers. Such is the basic tenet of this chapter: an exploration of the particular creativity brought into being by reading and responding to novels, by the *experience* of novels.

What is the creativity of the novel and why is it important to English?

If the dominance of the verbal is under threat from the visual (Kress 2010), then the novel must stake a claim as to why it still occupies considerable space on the curriculum. One possible assertion as to its continued and continuing importance is to see it not so much as *more* creative than other media but as *differently* creative in ways that are significant for young people's development and learning, not just as they come to terms with the forms most present in their daily lives – where the moving image would presumably trump the written word in most cases – but as they develop ways of bringing meaning to the world. This requires consideration of how different modes are received and processed by the mind. A *telling* mode, such as narrative writing, requires us to *conceive* of meaning, in other words to imagine it into being, whereas a *showing* mode, such as the moving image, requires us to *perceive* of meaning, or to notice it (Hutcheon 2006: 130). This is not to diminish the skills needed to 'read' images, but it is to suggest that in terms of creativity and meaning-making it takes a more considerable effort to read words, *conceiving* perhaps being a more cognitively demanding activity than *perceiving*. The novel, as a form that actively seeks to engage in verbal creativity and that places substantial demands on readers in terms of reading time, recall of content and making connections between various strands, would appear to stand as a special case for any exploration of creativity.

Reader-response theory (Iser 1978; Fish 1990) and a *theory of transactional reading* (Rosenblatt 1978) offer useful approaches for exploring the verbal creativity of the novel. The former is perhaps misleadingly named, for while it stresses the role of the reader in the construction of textual meaning, its chief proponents are clear that texts in turn *guide* readers towards particular responses. It has led to misunderstandings and misuses of the theory, critics lazily maintaining that it relativises all texts, leaving readers to claim as much meaning for *The Highway Code* as *Hamlet*.

This is in spite of Iser (1978: 107) constructing a frame in which "textual models and strategies" guide readers towards particular responses, and Fish (1990: 307) pointing out that it is impossible to assert "an infinite plurality of meanings" for any writing, given that all language is used within a particular context. Such mis-understanding perhaps makes Rosenblatt's (1978) *theory of transactional reading* a more attractive one to refer to here, for its name, borrowed from Dewey's collapsing of boundaries between, for example, the curriculum and the child (1920) and art and experience (2005 [1934]), acknowledges that any reading must simultaneously consider *what a text does to a reader* and *what a reader does to a text*. Transactional reading, then, acknowledges the creativity of both author and reader, though makes it clear they are not the same thing. Thus Rosenblatt warns against both awarding the reader "the reflected glory of duplicating the author's initial creativity" (49) and "[t]he view that the reader in re-creating the work re-enacts the author's creative role"; instead she stresses "the reader's own unique form of literary creativity" (50). The writer might guide the reader to a particular response, but it is the reader who makes that response in his or her unique way at the transactional point where prior experience meets with the experience of what is read. What follows is an attempt to categorise various aspects of creativity to be found in the *experience* of reading a novel, rooted in the notion that it is a transactional process.

The creativity of the aesthetic

Rosenblatt (1978: 23–27) distinguishes between *efferent* and *aesthetic* reading. The former is reading that seeks to extract information from a text. It might apply to recipes, or instructions, or a history book. The focus is not on the experience of reading but on what is gleaned from the process. In the latter the "primary concern is with what happens *during* the actual reading event" (24). The focus is all on experience, on what the text *does* to the reader and, consequently, what the reader can choose to *do* with the text. This is particularly important for English teachers as it provides a clear rationale for studying literary texts in different ways to non-literary ones. They need not worry about trying to explain to students why a novel is different to a science textbook, but instead encourage them to *do* different things with the former compared to the latter, and to consider how it *does* different things as it acts on them. Rosenblatt's work is based around reading poetry, but novels, in their size and scope, offer an extensive range of aesthetic experiences for classroom use.

The creativity of time

Part of what makes the aesthetic experience of reading a novel unique is the amount of time it takes. The need to engage with "the movingness of texts" (Fish 1990: 44), so that what has been read is constantly re-evaluated as further reading takes place, means the experience is not fixed but changes, develops – is created.

The creativity of the whole

Vygotsky (1986 [1936]) tells us that the sense of a complex text, and everything associated with it, can be accessed by the inner speech of the mind as a single word or phrase. Everything that an individual who has read the whole novel senses about *Bleak House* is contained within the title. When the individual begins to write about the novel or to talk to others then the sense is released in a "shower of words" (251). Novels, because of their size and potential for complexity, are particularly effective resources when considering the creativity of the whole. They contain not so much a shower of words as a deluge.

The creativity of absence

When the process of reading is made conscious, awareness is drawn as much to what is absent from a text as to what is present. The gaps in novels are an integral part of the act of conceiving. As readers imagine the world presented to them by the words on the page, so they imagine worlds beyond those words, whether consciously omitted by the author or not.

Transformative creativity

It is a truism to say that novels transport readers to other worlds. However, in the juxtaposition of a reader's own experience with that contained within a written narrative, a case can be made for the *transformative* creativity of the novel. It is transformative not just in the sense that, in the moment of reading, an individual's imagination is taken to new places, but also in the way that the world contained within a book will shift a reader's perceptions of his or her own world, even if in tiny, imperceptible ways. This is particularly applicable to young readers, with the possibilities afforded by youth analogous to those afforded by the novel form: ones of becoming, of creating and of being created. Consequently many novels for young people actively seek "to provoke the ultimate response of childhood, 'Why?' 'Why are things as they are?' 'Why can't they be different?'" (Reynolds 2007: 3).

Extending the vocabulary of creativity

For all their obvious appeal to English teaching, Rosenblatt's ideas, while not ignored, were not pushed to the fore during the latter part of the last century. Instead, they were sidelined in many progressive teaching circles by a focus on critical literacy (Peim 1993; Morgan 1996; Lankshear 1997), which itself sought to challenge traditional ways of looking at literature, by opening English up to a broader notion of textual study. The focus was successful in many ways and in England is embodied in the 'critical understanding' strand of the National Curriculum (QCDA 2007). However, in seeking to unmask the ideological underpinnings behind texts, it tended to ignore the *experience* of reading in order to reclaim them for particular political and social agendas. Consequently "it pushed affective texts like literature into the 'naughty corner'" (Goodwyn in Dean and Barton 2011). Put bluntly, it took the fun out of the subject. The study of literature was not about expanding horizons and looking at the world in new and exciting ways; it was about understanding the social forces that shaped the construction of texts, whether literary or not.

Perhaps confronting the paradox that English teachers were left having to promote reading for pleasure while denying students a sense of that pleasure, the last decade or so has given rise to theoretical work that seeks to reclaim the aesthetic, using it in the same way as Dewey and Rosenblatt, but also taking on board contemporary notions of identity, subjectivity and multiculturalism. This includes work on art in general (Armstrong 2000), literature as a whole (Attridge 2004) and English teaching specifically (Misson and Morgan 2006, 2007; Alexander 2007; Ellis, Fox and Street 2007). The chapter draws on this work next in setting out various activities that exploit the creativity of the novel. In many ways what follows does not extend particularly beyond the *theory of transactional reading* already set out, but it is used here not just because it is more contemporary, but because it offers a vocabulary useful for discussing the teaching of literature (as experience) in general.

Vocabulary point no. 1: textualness/authoredness

Misson and Morgan (2007) suggest that when English teachers approach texts they tend to focus on action and content, missing opportunities to explore "the texturing of texts" (76). This is the process by which texts come to be recognised as such; for example, the means by which a crime novel comes to be seen as a crime novel or a romance as a romance. It accepts that a text is structured to engage readers in particular choices and asks how this occurs. As such it focuses on the creativity of the text: both how it is put together and how it encourages responses. In similar fashion Attridge (2004) coins the term "authoredness" to refer to the conscious acts of creativity involved in writing literature and the identifiable markers of an individual writer. If you like, a novel becomes 'textured' with a particular writer's imprint. Both terms acknowledge that authors consciously seek to position their readers in particular ways, but that they can never fully be in control of this process. Boxes 5.1 and 5.2 offer example of how to teach for *textualness/authoredness*.

BOX 5.1 Hot-seating the author

Hot-seating is used regularly to engage students with the characters in a novel. While this shows students that texts can have an existence beyond the page, it does not build an understanding of how and why characters have been created as they are, or of the more general choices made by the author in 'texturing the text'. By hot-seating the author – a role usefully played by the teacher – students can consider how the author has written for particular effect and also how the text might bear his or her particular imprimatur, or 'authoredness'. In one way the author is made more real by the task; in another he or she enters the same kind of fictional realm as his or her characters. Thus students can see that all writing is created in some way by an individual, but that meaning can never entirely be traced back to his or her original intentions.

Readers might like to consider a familiar text to which they could respond in role to the following:

- Why is the main character a boy/girl?
- Why have you written in the first/third person?
- Why have you set the novel in the UK/abroad?
- Why have you written the book in the past/present/future?
- What age did you write for?
- Tell us about why the novel begins as it does.
- Did you cut anything from the novel that was originally there?
- Explain some of the vocabulary and style choices in your writing.
- Tell us how you came up with ideas for the ending of the novel.

BOX 5.2 Marketing a novel

While it is common classroom practice to explore audience when looking at films, it is less so with novels. Much work, for example, is done on the promotion of films, generally through creating posters or trailers, yet attention to the marketing of novels rarely extends beyond designing a front cover and writing a blurb. Such an omission limits students in understanding the whole process by which a novel is created: that it does not just involve writers and readers but publishers and buyers. Such a notion might seem to move away from ideas about 'textualness' and 'authoredness', but directing students to think carefully about potential readership leads them to consider the particular qualities of what has been read: how it reaches out to particular audiences and how its author can be distinguished from others. A range of activities can help students engage with the identification and creation of audience:

- Designing a marketing poster rather than a book cover.
- Storyboarding and, if possible, creating an internet 'trailer' for the book. This is occasionally done by publishers to promote high-profile books and examples can be found on publisher websites.
- Interviewing the author about why people should read his or her book.
- Storyboarding and, if possible, creating a trailer for a film adaptation of the book. This task differs from creating an internet trailer promoting the book, as it challenges readers to consider the differences in 'textualness' between books and films: what makes a book a book and a film a film? It also raises issues about 'authoredness', including the challenging question as to whether or not a film can be authored.

Vocabulary point no. 2: ethics/otherness

Teachers are familiar with encouraging students to impose different interpretations on texts. For example, it is common practice to ask small groups to explore a text from a particular point of view. Among older readers this might involve taking on quite complex critical stances, such those offered by Marxism, Feminism or Psychoanalysis. Younger students might be encouraged to look at a text from more straightforward points of view; for example, to look at it as an older reader, or as a reader of the opposite sex, as a teacher or as a parent. The task encourages a creativity of response: students develop and are exposed to a range of possible meanings, expanding on their own critical awareness as the process goes on. It also allows students to confront *ethical* aspects of a text as they explore what it means to different readers, creating as they go along what might be considered "a *communal identity*" (Kearney 1988: 395). Such a task, though, still relies predominantly on what readers do to texts. An approach to creativity that also takes into account what a text does to readers needs to think not only about how texts help readers to become *ethical beings* but also how they manipulate readers to accept certain *ethical stances*. Attridge (2004) considers this symbiotic text–reader relationship when exploring what he calls the "alterity" and "otherness" of literature. He does not use the terms to refer to cultural or social *others* against whom a dominant group can define itself; rather he uses it to suggest that literature develops our understanding of the world through offering a new perspective on it. Thus literature always moves towards *otherness* in that it presents readers with a world that can never exactly be their own, even as, in reading it, it enters in some way into their realm of experience. This applies equally to novels that construct fantastic worlds of the imagination and ones that draw on familiar, contemporary surroundings (52). Boxes 5.3 and 5.4 outline possible activities to enable students to engage with the ethics and otherness of novels, to experience what Attridge terms "an encounter with alterity" (27).

BOX 5.3 Holding a novel to trial

Students rarely get to choose what novels are read in class. They are then often denied passing explicit judgement on them, instead being directed to comment on linguistic or structural features. Such tasks deny direct engagement with novels and risk removing them from the real, lived experience of young readers. Holding a trial for a book addresses this in two ways. It allows students to consider why a book might be considered worth reading (its *ethical* value) and it encourages reflection on the different responses the book might stimulate (in *others*). At its simplest, the task can be structured so as to pass judgement on whether or not the novel in question is worthy of classroom study. Half of the class argue in defence of the novel, the other half against. In planning, prosecution and defence can consider the following:

- why students like or dislike the novel;
- the educational value of the novel;
- the presentation of life in the novel;
- the suitability of the novel's content and characters for the particular class;
- the likely responses of different students to the novel depending on their own backgrounds;
- the reasons teachers might think it is suitable for study;
- the level of challenge offered by the novel.

BOX 5.4 How does a novel make you *feel*?

A key ethical consideration when reading a novel must be how it makes readers *feel* (or *not* feel, as the case may be). This might appear trivial, but it is key to emphasising that novels do act on readers and that readers can act in their turn, depending on how a novel has affected them. It is also a useful starting point for a range of other activities. For once students have been allowed to engage with their emotional responses, they might well be more confident in discussing other aspects of the text.

Questions like the ones below can be used as stimuli. Students can be directed to answer as themselves or, if exploring *otherness*, in role.

- Do you like this book? Why/why not?
- In what ways does this book relate to your life?
- Are you glad you read this book? Why/why not?
- Which character in the book do you relate to most and why?
- Which character do you like least and why?
- If you could change one thing about this book what would it be?
- What message, if any, do you take away from this book?

Vocabulary point no. 3: text as event

Attridge (2004) encourages us to treat literature as, in part, an 'event' (a term also used by Rosenblatt), an acknowledgement that the creativity of a text cannot always be controlled, but evolves according to how it is experienced. Thus the "creation of the text" (26) depends both on willed endeavours and unplanned happenings, occurring both as "something that is done intentionally by an effort of the will" and as "something that happens without warning to a passive, though alert, consciousness". It is never simply one or the other.

Classroom activities (see Boxes 5.5 to 5.7) can mirror the simultaneity of literature as act and event in allowing students consciously to manipulate the material given to them in ways designed to bring into being unexpected results. Thus they engage with what a text is *trying to do* and as a consequence *make it do* something that cannot be anticipated.

BOX 5.5 Video journals

This task draws on the concept of "the movingness of texts" (Fish 1990: 44). Teachers have long encouraged students to keep reading journals, tracking their responses to developments in a novel. New digital technologies enable an even closer engagement with how meaning is created in keeping pace with a narrative's development. Digital video enables students to respond immediately to what is read and easily share their ideas with others, both in the moment and over the entire period of reading. If different students respond on video after each section, the recorded clips can be shown in sequence once a book is finished. Thus students get to experience and re-experience their collective impressions of a novel. For the clips to make sense in sequence, each recording needs to begin with a brief précis of plot before offering comments on the section in question.

BOX 5.6 Instant re-creation

Rather than being asked to give an emotional or analytical response after each section of a novel is read, as in Box 5.5, students can be directed to re-enact the passages instead. This can be done in a relatively static way, relying on dialogue only, or it can involve physically acting out a scene. The teacher records one group's response after each reading. Each is then saved and played in sequence when the novel is finished, allowing the class to experience how their own re-creations shift as the narrative develops.

BOX 5.7 Tableaux

Tableaux offer a simple way for students to experience a particular moment in a text. Key to the success of the technique is in asking students to comment on the emotions being felt by characters. Responses can be drawn from students observing others in a tableau or by characters coming out of their freeze-frame positions one at a time to comment on how they are feeling. Another innovative strategy is to treat a tableau as a museum piece. Students observe a group frozen in position as if they are an exhibit in a museum. In silence the observers make notes on the exhibit. These notes then inform writing a poem about what has been seen. Thus a class get to experience a text in multiple forms – novel to tableau to poem – each offering and requiring a different response and each overtly transforming the text into an *event*.

Creativity, class-readers and choice

The creativity of children's fiction is not a given. Jacqueline Rose's (1993) land-mark study of the subject, *The Case of Peter Pan, or the Impossibility of Children's*

Fiction argues that writing for children is an adult construct that maintains a separation between adults and children, fixing the latter in time in an idealised, adult version of youth. Peter Pan, the boy who literally does not grow up, provides the template for her argument, which sets children's literature firmly within the realm of "compliance" (Winnicott 1971). Children are just that, children, with no possibility of moving beyond their adult-imposed identity. Rose's work is effectively challenged by Kimberley Reynolds (2007) in *Radical Children's Literature: Future visions and aesthetic transformations in juvenile fiction*. She heralds "the future orientation" (3) of many novels for young people as indicative of the role they can play in "filling the minds of generations of young readers with experiences, emotions, and the mental furniture and tools necessary for thinking about themselves and the world they inhabit" (1). Certainly, she acknowledges that much fiction for young people has a conformist orientation (68), but stresses that the work she focuses on positions young people in a state of becoming, in many cases moving through different stages of childhood, creating their identity as they go along. A good example would be David Almond's (2011) *My Name is Mina*, the sequel to his much taught *Skellig* (1998). Mina, a school-refuser, is educated by her mother at home. From the start, then, readers are given access to a realm likely to be outside their own experience. Within the book, Mina explores her own identity, the novel structured as a kind of journal containing her thoughts on her current life, reflections on her past, short stories and poems. Through various textual entries she constructs her sense of *self*. Always, though, there is the presence of outside forces acting on her, particularly the prospect of having, one day, to return to school. Thus the book explores how a young girl creates her own identity within the social confines of her life. It also stands as an interesting example of meta-fiction. Readers who have previously encountered *Skellig* will be aware that Mina befriends that novel's central protagonist, Michael. Thus any meaning taken from the prequel is infused with a sense of the earlier work. This draws attention to the book as a work of fiction, but, in explicitly being about a young girl's creativity and creation of self, it also results in the possibility of drawing an analogy between the process of becoming as constructed in a novel and the process of actual becoming in life: fictional creation and self-creation are clearly linked.

While *My Name is Mina* offers readers an insight into a young girl exploring a range of subjectivities – and so offers them insight into creating their own identities – it does not necessarily follow that they will be interested in her story. This taps into one of the biggest problems faced in teaching a class reader. While the choice of text can have a significant impact on learning and creativity, it is unlikely that any novel will generate the same level of affective response in all readers, or chime significantly with their own prior experience. The problem can be offset in some ways by structuring activities around the *experience* of the novel, as explored above, accepting that this does not have to be positive. A happier solution, however, would give students some choice in their reading matter. Doing this is very much dependent on the resources available and requires a greater degree of planning, but is possible (see Box 5.8). If, as argued, creativity and learning both stem in part from the interaction between how the prior experience of young people interacts with new material, then the new material needs to resonate as much as possible with individual readers, whether it is giving them access to entirely new worlds, or providing them with fresh insight into familiar territory. If no interest is generated then creativity and learning are unlikely to follow.

BOX 5.8 Voting on which novel to read next

At its most basic an experiential approach allows students to say whether or not they like a novel. The next step, to give reasons for liking or not liking, is not so straightforward and, in some ways, contradicts the notion of experiencing. For the reason might lie in a *sense* of the text, an imprecise notion that is difficult for young readers to articulate. While one role of the English teacher is to help students to articulate their thoughts, individual readers might, with some justification, be resistant to such pressures: I like it because I do! A route beyond the limitations of a like/dislike approach lies in the exploration of preferences. Introducing a comparative element to literary study enables both affective and critical responses to be framed within specific terms of textual reference. For example, it is easier to say why you prefer one thing to another than to simply say why you like something: the former provides a ready-made context in which to make statements while the latter relies upon an unspecified prior textual knowledge that may not exist.

While there is rarely time to explore two novels within a scheme of work, it is possible to investigate the openings to a range of novels in a single lesson. This can even be done with the intention of allowing students to vote on the best opening in order to continue reading that book. It could also form the start of a scheme of work in which small groups each read a different book of their choice. This would be particularly manageable if students were all looking at the same genre. For example, a class could explore the openings to four spy novels aimed at a teenage audience. Individually they could select which novel to continue as part of a scheme based on the genre, everyone in the class carrying out the same activities but on a range of novels. This approach would require a department to have a wide range of sets of novels available. However, it can also be applied to short stories that can easily be photocopied.

A possible selection process is outlined below. It enables students to see how a novel begins to create meaning from the very first word and also how they bring their own meaning to everything they read. It uses novels from the AQA GCSE English Literature specification for 2011, thus making the bold suggestion that students might actually be able to choose their own exam texts!

1. Students are given the opening sentence to six novels. Having discussed each sentence in small groups, the class vote on which one to reject. Titles and authors are provided here for teachers but would be withheld from students.

When he was nearly thirteen, my brother Jem got his arm badly broken at the elbow.

Harper Lee, *To Kill a Mockingbird*

My name is Francis Joseph Cassavant and I have just returned to Frenchtown in Monument and the war is over and I have no face.

Robert Cormier, *Heroes*

A few miles south of Soledad the Salinas River drops in close to the hillside bank and runs deep and green.

John Steinbeck, *Of Mice and Men*

If you really want to hear about it, the first thing you'll probably want to know is where I was born, and what my lousy childhood was like, and how my parents were occupied and all before they had me, and all that David Copperfield kind of crap, but I don't feel like going into it, if you want to know the truth.

J. D. Salinger, *Catcher in the Rye*

The boy with the fair hair lowered himself down the last few feet of rock and began to pick his way towards the lagoon.

William Golding, *Lord of the Flies*

Hooper had known, from the very first moment he had looked into Kingshaw's face, that it would all be easy, that he would always be able to make him afraid.

Susan Hill, *I'm the King of the Castle*

2. Students are given the next sentence to the five remaining novels. Discussion resumes before a second is rejected.

3 – 5. The process continues until only one novel remains.

The task in Box 5.8 forces students to engage with the creativity of novels in all sorts of ways. For in articulating preferences they need to compare various elements of each extract. They also need to speculate as to how the novels might continue and react to subsequent lines as they appear. They are simultaneously required to bring their own responses to the openings to bear, articulating why they do or don't like them, how they think they will continue, why they do or don't want to read on, etc., while also reflecting on how the creativity of each generates particular responses.

Conclusion

The novel occupies a curious position in the English curriculum. It takes up a great deal of space and yet is often used, particularly when teaching a text for exams, in limited ways: in the worst cases as little more than a source for demonstrating the ability to comment critically on various linguistic and structural features. At the heart of this practice is the act of interpretation: the novel is read in a literal way and then mined for alternative, *deeper* meanings. In a sense this act of interpretation can be seen as a form of *re*-creativity. The text begins as one thing and becomes another. However, I would argue that too narrow a focus on interpretation limits creativity, taking away the experiential aspect of reading. A creative approach always remains in touch with the original. It begins with an acknowledgement that reading is an *experience* and, consequently, the text acts upon the reader as the reader acts upon the novel. Creativity comes from both sides in a *transactional* process. The original never stays the same, for even when the physical text is unchanged, every reading – and the simple passage of time itself – works upon it in some way. It is in a continual state of creation.

Too narrow a focus on interpretation also moves young readers away from what novels can *do* – both by intentional *act* and by incidental *event*. It is to the *aesthetic* experience of novels that teachers must turn if they are to exploit the potential in novels for learning through creativity. For active engagement with a narrative brings with it, among other things, possibilities for an engagement with *otherness*, for an awareness of *ethics*, for the contemplation of choice, for an understanding of how subjectivities are shaped and for articulating the world in new and emboldened ways.

Key texts

Attridge, D. (2004) *The singularity of literature*. London and New York: Routledge.

Misson, R. and Morgan, W. (2007) 'How critical is the aesthetic? The role of literature in English', in V. Ellis, C. Fox and B. Street, *Rethinking English in schools*. London and New York: Continuum, pp. 73–87.

Rosenblatt, L. (1978) *The reader, the text, the poem: The transactional theory of the literary work*. Carbondale, IL: Southern Illinois University Press.

6

Listening, reading and creativity

Dwelling in every written text there are voices.
David Toop, *Sinister Resonance: The Mediumship of Listening*

Can one *make a listening listened to*?

Peter Szendy, *Listen: A History of our Ears*

Listening presents itself as passive. Sit back and listen. Just listen. Easy listening. Active listening would seem to be oxymoronic. How can we actively do something that cannot be avoided in the first place? One might as well talk of active breathing as of active listening. Listening is not optional; we cannot close our ears. It just happens.

And yet listening lies at the heart of creativity and learning. If human creativity and learning have their origins in the evolution of language (Mithen 1996; Tomasello 1999), then the means of receiving that language – listening – must be as important as the means of delivering it – talking. Perhaps the silence involved in most reading, along with the connotations it holds as a trusted route to learning, has relegated listening to a subsidiary role. Reading takes effort and is done for a specific purpose, listening simply takes place. This chapter seeks to collapse distinctions between the two, portraying them as analogous to one another. It does so to highlight the multiple functions of both practices and their importance as processing points for working on the material of creativity and learning. For reading does not just involve the eye receiving written text; it requires transforming what is read into inner speech, *listening* to a text with due consideration for possible sounds present in the written word, be it the rhythms and cadences of poetry, the voices contained in written dialogue, or the authorial presence within any piece of writing. And in listening we do not simply hear a series of sounds that convey a particular meaning no matter where they come from. We also *read* what we hear. So in the case of speech, we *read* the voice behind words, with consideration for accent, tone and cadence and for traces of all the previous instances when we have been exposed to those same words and the voices that uttered them. To gain a full understanding, then, both of what we hear and what we read, involves a good deal of effort. Active reading necessitates active listening and vice versa.

That reading and listening are inextricably linked is borne out in the first word of the first great work of English literature to be written down. "Hwaet," translatable as "Listen," says the narrator of *Beowulf*. The word draws notice to the epic poem's oral story-telling roots, but it also demands attention: readers must be listeners and listeners must be readers, each actively processing what is presented to them. This link between reading and listening has been neglected by English practitioners in recent decades, as has the activity of listening itself. Chapters in textbooks for English teachers (Brindley 1994; Davison and Moss 2000; Clarke, Dickinson and Westbrook 2009; Davison and Dowson 2009) claiming to focus on 'speaking and listening' rarely deal with anything other than the former, and pedagogical investigations into 'dialogic talk' (Wells 1986; Mercer 1995; Mercer and Hodgkinson 2007; Alexander, R. 2008) are plentiful but on 'dialogic listening' virtually non-existent. The neglect of listening within work on dialogic practices is indicative of an imbalance in approaches to classroom material; they promote the need for young people to respond to texts, but without necessarily giving them sufficient time or direction to receive that material in the first place: to read it *and* to listen to it.

This chapter explores how creativity occurs in the transition between receiving a text – to be taken here as a hybrid of reading and listening – and commenting on it, or re-creating it in some shape or form. In other words it takes place in the transformation from outer to inner speech and then, optionally, back to outer speech again (Vygotsky 1986 [1936]). The more effective the processes of listening to what is read and reading what is listened to, the greater the potential for creativity and for learning. The work on dialogic talk alluded to above has convincingly demonstrated the advances in learning that take place when students are able to discuss material presented to them in structured, non-hierarchical conditions. The focus of such work is very much on the new knowledge that is demonstrably brought into being through what is actually articulated in the classroom. Yet there is clearly an element of dialogic practice that does not require talk. Active reading and listening are dialogic in nature, but can evoke responses held in the mind as inner speech. The processing that takes place in the mind is as important to learning as any articulated response. And yet very little attention is paid to this in structuring lessons. Emphasis instead is given to the material given to students and to their actual responses, ignoring what occurs in between. The focus here is on the 'in between'. This means encouraging learners to reflect on how they read and listen, so cultivating ways of *listening to their listening* (Szendy 2008) and drawing attention to the parallels between reading and listening.

The chapter is divided into three sections: one that looks at "reading with the ear" (Alexander, J. 2008), one that involves listening to how others read and one that develops a 'critical listening' approach to written texts.

Reading with the ear

Joy Alexander (2008) offers the possibility of a paradigm shift in the way listening is viewed within the English curriculum. She argues that instead of organising the "profile components" of English so that 'reading' goes with 'writing' and 'speaking' with 'listening', as is the case in England's *National Curriculum Programme of Study for English* (QCDA 2007), it is more useful to pair 'writing' with 'speaking' and 'reading' with 'listening'. To give force to her argument, she explains that listening was given a much higher profile in the early years of English as a school subject than it is today, to the extent that a 1937 Board of Education document states that "English, in short, is on the one side listening and reading, on the other side speaking and writing" (in Alexander, J. 2008: 221). This particular pattern remains largely unchallenged until the 1960s when work on helping young people develop their speaking skills (Wilkinson 1965) leads to a reconfiguration into *speaking and listening* (or 'oracy') and *reading and writing* (or 'literacy').

This arrangement has since been largely unchallenged. At first, Alexander's call for realignment appears regressive. Her argument relies on appealing for students to read more material out loud, a practice that evokes images of drilled, rote learning, largely abandoned with the rise of oracy on the grounds that it bears little relation to everyday language use (222). However, aligning 'listening' with 'speaking' has, effectively, led to it being ignored in classroom practice. This is manifested in what Alexander refers to as a "rush to meaning" (228), whereby teachers, in part driven by pressures to teach to objectives and to guarantee exam success, deny students the opportunity to engage with texts on their own terms. Instead textual work becomes little more than a search for structural and linguistic devices, so that the teaching of poetry, for example, focuses heavily either on form (sonnet, narrative poem, rhyming couplets, etc.) or the use of language (metaphor, simile, etc.) (227). Alexander reaches back all the way to George Sampson's 1922 *English for the English* to develop her point further, borrowing his phrase "creative reception" to advocate a more student-centred approach that sees understanding texts as evolving through multiple readings and "reading with the ear" (225). While she interprets Sampson's use of "creative reception" in very different terms to how it is perceived in Chapter 1 of this book (where it is deemed to refer to a passive rather than active response), it is a useful term in considering how texts as a whole work on readers and how readers, in turn, work on texts. Alexander makes the point that "[t]rite as it may appear, we learn to read poetry by reading poems" (227) and that "focusing the attention on hearing the poem through having to read it aloud simultaneously facilitates understanding of, and insight into, the poem" (227). The activities in Boxes 6.1 to 6.5 build on Alexander's ideas about pairing 'reading' and 'listening', in ways that encourage students to reflect on what they hear when they read in order better to understand the creativity of the reading material and to generate greater complexity and comprehension in their own responses.

BOX 6.1 Reading for sense before meaning

This activity combines Vygotsky's (1986 [1936]: 247) ideas about whole texts existing in the mind as *sense* with Joy Alexander's (2008: 232) about "reading with the ear". Its staged approach encourages students to read without worrying about what a poem means, while alerting them to ways that meaning emerges as it becomes more familiar. Students build up a *sense* of the poem from several different sources and viewpoints before their thoughts have gathered a critical mass sufficient to emerge as a "shower of words" (Vygotsky 1986 [1936]: 251). They are developing their own *creative* response, in that it evolves and shifts with time and additional stimuli.

Stage 1: Give students a poem to read to themselves. Ask them to think as little as possible about meaning but to listen to how the poem sounds in their heads. Allow time for several readings.

Stage 2: Read the poem out loud to the whole class. Ask for a continued focus on sound rather than meaning. Take care that there is no actual discussion of the poem but instead ask students to reflect in silence about how the reading compares to what they 'heard' earlier in their heads.

Stage 3: Direct groups of four to construct a reading of the poem to present to the rest of the class based on their different 'hearings'. Ask groups to discuss the various parts of the poem carefully before developing their group reading. At this stage a mixture of references to meaning will begin to emerge.

Stage 4: Listen to group readings of the poem. When this is finished ask for comments about the different versions. Ask for reflection on how each reading alters the possible meaning of the poem. After that, encourage further reflection, either through discussion or writing, about what the poem means. As part of this direct students to consider how meaning develops and changes with various readings: in other words, how meaning is created at the meeting point of the voices in the poem, the voices in their own heads, and the voices of classmates.

Stage 5: Offer students additional ideas about the poem that might add to those they have developed themselves. Give them the opportunity to accept, reject or modify these ideas.

BOX 6.2 Asking questions about a text

Direct students to read a poem (this activity could also easily work with a range of other types of text) in silence. As with the previous activity, ask for a focus on what the reading 'sounds' like in their heads. On a second reading direct them to ask questions of the poem while reading it, thus consciously engaging with its dialogic nature. They should write the questions down beside the text. These can be on a very simplistic level, such as asking what a particular word means, or they can be more sophisticated, asking, for example, about particular word choices, the selection of subject matter, or gaps in the poem. As teacher, take the questions from the class. This can be done in role as the poem's author, or as a linguistic or literary expert. Ask students to record responses in a suitable format. For example, the session could be treated as a news conference, or it could simply be an opportunity to gather ideas for a formal written response.

An alternative approach is to join students up into pairs or small groups after they have asked questions of the poem individually. They can try to answer each other's questions, leaving any unanswered ones for the hot-seating exercise.

BOX 6.3 Sound tunnels

At times it is useful to look at some of the constituent parts of a text before reading the whole; for example, when a piece is rich in language designed to provoke a particular emotion. Sound tunnels work particularly well with short poems, emotionally charged passages from dramatic texts and key descriptive extracts from novels.

Give students a line each from a poem or a short phrase or sentence from a piece of prose or drama. Ask them to select an interesting or evocative word or phrase. Place them in two equally sized lines facing one another to make a 'sound tunnel'. Students at one end of the tunnel peel off to walk through the tunnel. The other students say their word or phrase out loud as their classmates pass. When a student gets to the end of the tunnel, they rejoin the line and the next student starts walking. From what they hear they will get a sense of the richness of vocabulary in the text they are about to read. You can direct them to say words in a particular tone (and it is always useful to suggest whispering the word to avoid excessive noise). Those walking through the tunnel can also do so with their eyes closed to achieve a heightened sense of listening. In this instance ask them to stand with their arms stretched in front of them, so that walkers can gently be guided along.

BOX 6.4 Poem as sound

There are a number of ways to draw links to the musical and rhythmic qualities of poetry. The two examples here focus on developing a *sense* of a poem before addressing its meaning.

1. *Poetry as percussion*: direct students to turn a poem, no matter how long or short, into a thirty- to sixty-second percussion performance. If instruments are unavailable or not practical for classroom use, draw on any available resources (i.e. things to hit and bang!). To limit sound, instruct students to clap and tap using no more than two fingers. The activity draws students' attention towards how meaning is constructed from rhythm and tone as well as vocabulary.

2. *Soundtrack to a poem*: ask small groups to decide on a piece of music to accompany a poem. Direct them to articulate why the music is suitable, and then move on to selecting images to go with the poem. The images are flashed up alongside the poem in a PowerPoint presentation (or using more sophisticated editing software if time permits). As in previous activities, this is useful in developing the *sense* of a poem before moving on to its meaning. The activity is particularly effective if each group has a different poem. They can then be introduced to each other's poems as pure *sense*, with no awareness of the words themselves. The presentations can then be adapted by writing the words alongside the images, or by reading them out loud over the images and soundtrack.

BOX 6.5 Sound modelling

Models are used regularly to guide students through writing tasks. While useful in alerting students to patterns and conventions, they can limit creativity, leading to excessive reliance on examples and a simple copying with minor variations. An alternative approach is to give students *sound models* as a way into writing. In other words, they listen to the example of what they are to write rather than read it. Writing in the style of the model then involves recalling patterns of rhythm and sound as well as vocabulary and punctuation rather than simply copying them. It can work with formal and informal texts, but is particularly effective when students need to write texts, such as speeches, specifically for oral delivery. Short models are most effective, as they can easily be listened to several times, with key aspects of rhythm recalled in entirety.

Listening to how others read

'Reading with the ear' helps learners engage with the creativity of a text. By consciously imagining how the words on a page might sound out loud, they gain insight into how they are directed to 'hear' in a particular way, but also into how they themselves can construct a particular 'hearing'. They are able to do so because of the dialogic nature of language. All language use exists in relation to other language use, so that any 'utterance' is part of "a very complexly organised chain of other utterances" (Bakhtin 2006: 69). *Active listening* involves locating language within this chain, contemplating the connotations of meaning available within the context of the entire system of language. Bakhtin explains how we always have different choices available when listening, albeit often in the form of an instantaneous reaction and so not open to conscious reflection:

> The fact is that when the listener perceives and understands the meaning (the language meaning) of speech, he simultaneously takes an active, responsive attitude toward it. He either agrees or disagrees with it (completely or partially), augments it, applies it, prepares for its execution, and so on.
>
> (68)

In the classroom creativity and learning can be enhanced by opening up as many different responses to texts as possible; in other words in enabling students to hear and learn from each other. Each time something new is said, the rest of the class is able to "take an active, responsive attitude". In other words, by listening to all the other voices in a classroom, students constantly modify their own. In many ways such listening is *instinctive*. Box 6.6 explores a task that deliberately draws attention to how learners can listen to one another so that it also becomes *reflective*.

BOX 6.6 Listening to the author's voice

One impediment to active listening lies in the relationship between teachers and learners. In their desire for approval, learners do not necessarily give all their attention to a text, but to what they think a teacher wants to hear about it (Mercer 1995). Consequently responses are limited, reflecting the perceived, singular interests of the teacher's voice, rather than the multiple interests of a whole class.

Requiring students to respond in role helps to address this problem. To a certain degree it removes anxieties about getting things wrong: any mistakes are down to the character being role-played. Consequently students begin to explore a greater variety of responses. The following example places students in the role of the writer. This forces them to engage with a

---

text at the point of its composition rather than as it becomes a tool for classroom learning. They are also encouraged, initially, to focus on what they *like* about it, which enables a more *affective* response and removes anxiety they might feel about what a poem *means*. While referring to poetry, the example can be applied to all manner of texts. It is structured in stages in a similar way to the 'Reading for sense before meaning' task above.

Stage 1: Students read a poem several times on their own, imagining they wrote it. In role as the writer, they think about what they particularly like about it, underlining and commenting on the three phrases or lines that please them most.

Stage 2: Still in role students think about the whole poem. They briefly write what the poem is about and why they wrote it, explaining how the three sections they identified in Stage 1 fit in with the overall design. In this way they combine a sense of the whole text with its individual moments.

Stage 3: In pairs students share their ideas. They write down a definitive list of three things they – as author – like most about the poem and a fifty- to hundred-word statement on what the poem is about and why they wrote it.

Stage 4: Pairs join into fours and compare notes. In this way they get to listen to the ideas of each other and develop their own. They discuss which pair has the most convincing version of what the real author might think. The responses of various groups should then be opened up to the whole class in order to extend the process of *dialogic listening* further.

Stage 5: Pairs write a three- to four-hundred-word magazine feature in the voice of the author, entitled "The Best Poem I Ever Wrote". Listen to a range of responses and ask for comments on how responses were developed by drawing on ideas from others.

Critical listening: voice and the class reader

When studying a novel, students are often directed towards a combination of close reading tasks and broader analytical activities that focus on, for example, themes or character. Study is firmly embedded in the *text*. The word itself draws attention to its print-based origins, no matter that it is regularly applied to all manner of phenomena: *the body as text, classroom as text, film as text*, etc. Classroom study tends to grapple with the text as a printed form. In other words, students look closely at the words on the page, perhaps discuss them, perhaps transform them into another form, and almost certainly try to understand and interpret them. How often, however, beyond an initial reading out loud, are the words worked upon to consider how they *sound*? Rarely, is the likely answer from most teachers. What follows introduces the term *critical listening* and considers how it might be used to explore the creativity of a novel, both in terms of how it might position itself to *sound* to its readers and how they, in turn, might construct their own *listening*. At the heart of critical listening is a belief that consciously listening to words – be it in the mind or as they are expressed out loud – provides additional insight into the power of a text and the range of meanings it makes available. Perhaps a useful analogy would be to compare any piece of writing to musical notation: the reader conducts a 'sound interpretation' of what is read. Dewey (2005 [1934]) makes this point about music when discussing the need to convince people that works of art take on new meaning each time they are experienced, even though they keep the same physical form across time: "no one doubts that the lines and dots on paper are more than the recorded means of evoking the work of art" (113). We are back to *Beowulf*. "Hwaet." "Listen." Creativity and learning lie in paying attention to how texts sound.

Elizabeth Laird's (2003) *A Little Piece of Ground* has been identified by a panel of children's writers as the best available example of young adult fiction "with a serious moral agenda" (Belbin 2011: 140). It focuses on the lives of three young Palestinian boys growing up in territory occupied by Israeli armed forces: Karim, a middle-class Muslim, Hopper, a Muslim living in the refugee camps and Joni, a middle-class Christian. It is not particularly widely read – and so listened to – and centres around a topic rarely discussed in classrooms. Whether or not book and topic should be more widely heard is not for me to dictate; but the choice is intended to provoke consideration of the subject matter we offer students in reading material, with a specific focus on how this, in turn, relates to listening and creativity.

In part creativity in this novel comes from the self-conscious way it places characters with everyday, ordinary interests in extraordinary settings. This encourages young readers to relate to the characters, but also forces them to take on roles well beyond their own experience. This juxtaposition of the everyday and the extraordinary can be exploited in asking students to develop readings of passages that combine both (see Box 6.7).

BOX 6.7 Reading the 'voices' in an extract

At the start of *A Little Piece of Ground* Karim writes a list of "The ten best things I want to do (or be) in my life". In pairs, decide how to read it out loud, developing a different style of voice for each point. Consider how the different voices suggest different roles that Karim has to take on in his life.

1. Champion footballer of the entire world (even I can dream).
2. Extremely cool, popular and good-looking and at least 1.90 metres tall (or anyway taller than Jamal).

3. The liberator of Palestine and a national hero.

4. Famous TV presenter or actor (famous, anyway).

5. Best-ever creator of new computer games.

6. My own person, allowed to do what I like without parents and big brothers and teachers on my back all the time.

7. Inventor of an acid formula to dissolve reinforced steel as used in tanks and helicopter gunships (Israeli ones).

8. Stronger than Joni and my other mates (this is not asking much).

9. Alive. Plus, if I have to get shot, only in places that heal up. Not in the head or spine, *inshallah*.

But number ten defeated him. He decided to keep the slot free in case a good idea should come to him later.

(1–2)

As the novel progresses, the everyday becomes increasingly intertwined with the extraordinary. For example, in one memorable scene Hopper swings playfully from the gun turret of a tank. In another he leaves an empty suitcase in a public place so that Israeli soldiers think it is a bomb. Along with Karim and Joni, he watches with a mixture of playfulness and seriousness as the soldiers carry out a controlled explosion of the suspected device. Tasks (for example Box 6.8) that encourage students to reproduce the dialogue of the boys give an insight into how meaning is generated through this curious juxtaposition. They have the potential to help students understand what might motivate young people living in war zones to behave in a morally conflicted way. They might also make students feel uncomfortable, questioning not only whether the boys should be doing such things, but also whether the author should be including them in a children's novel.

BOX 6.8 Reproducing dialogue

Karim, Hopper and Joni have a lot of fun during the course of the book, even though some of their activities are extremely dangerous and of questionable morality. In groups of three, re-create from memory conversations between the three boys based on one of the following:

■ clambering up scaffolding to watch the Israeli military try to defuse the fake bomb planted by Hopper;

- Hopper taunting the military by throwing an aubergine (shaped like a grenade) at a tank and then swinging from its gun turret;
- Karim hiding for two days in an abandoned car because he failed to get home during a curfew.

Part of *A Little Piece of Ground's* appeal is that it self-consciously acknowledges different viewpoints. Thus Palestinians are not reduced to a single entity but shown to be diverse in backgrounds, interests and faiths. While the three central characters unite in play, they also negotiate their friendship through the differences generated by their backgrounds. Readers are exposed to the creativity of these differences as each character constructs a different version of this unfamiliar world. By giving time and space to three distinct voices, the novel offers young readers insight into the complexity of the situation. There are many other voices in the book too, including those of people close to the boys such as parents, brothers, sisters and teachers, but also of young Israeli soldiers and of radio news broadcasts that regularly punctuate the text with reports of the fighting. Using the word 'voice' rather than character increases the sense of competing meanings in the text and in the region of Palestine as a whole. Readers gain an awareness of the need to navigate these differences while relating their own knowledge and understanding to them. They can use these disparate voices to create their own story of the region. Boxes 6.9 and 6.10 suggest activities that explore how meaning is created by the many voices present in the book, but also how a fuller understanding might also come from reflecting on which voices are not included, and why.

BOX 6.9 Exploring a range of voices

Write down as many different voices from *A Little Piece of Ground* as you can find (don't include the three central characters, Karim, Hopper and Joni). When you have finished draw conclusions about how complete a picture of Palestine is provided by this novel.

- Who do you want to hear from more?
- Who do you want to hear from not present in the novel?
- What more do you want to know?

BOX 6.10 Unheard voices

A Little Piece of Ground tells the story of three Palestinian boys and their families as they experience occupation by Israeli forces. The novel does not tell the story of all sides, though. For instance, we hear very little about why the Israeli government feels it has a right for its troops to be there. The book's publisher seems aware of this. At the front a positive review says:

'A partial account and easy to read but with a resonance that remains in the mind long after the book has been finished'

Carousel

Write down all the questions you need answered in order to get as full a picture as possible of what is going on.

Critical listening requires students consciously to listen to what they read in order to hear the voices that emanate from a text. They must also consciously reflect on how they think the novel might sound if read out loud. Novels, though, contain tens of thousands of words and multiple voices, making it impossible to hear everything, or to consciously project a voice on to everything. In combating this, teachers can alert students to look out for particular features in a text that will give them opportunities to reflect upon particular aspects of its construction. For example, students can be directed to listen for sounds, to hear noises as well as voices. *A Little Piece of Ground* is filled with noises that might easily be skimmed over in a conventional reading. Keeping a 'sound journal' is one way to draw attention to its 'soundscape'. Performances that draw on sounds as they are described (see Box 6.11) serve a similar function.

BOX 6.11 Performing sounds

Below is a small selection of noises from *A Little Piece of Ground*. Working in fours, select one or two words each. Develop a thirty-second performance using only the words selected to give an impression of the 'soundscape' in which Karim, Hopper and Joni live.

. . . they heard a crackle as the soldiers' loudspeaker cleared its throat and the awful, frightening rumble as the tanks came nearer and nearer up the hill.

> 'Whee! Bang! Gotcha!' the boy started shouting. 'Right on the gun turret! One soldier down! Three to go!'
>
> . . . bloodcurdling cries . . .
>
> Outside, there were occasional shouts, or the wailing of distant sirens, and, once or twice, more bursts of firing, but in between a sullen silence lay over the occupied city . . .
>
> . . . from the mosque below the refugee camp, the words of the evening prayer sounded out across the city.

One of the strengths of *A Little Piece of Ground* is that its range of voices makes it a *dialogic* text. While it offers its story from a Palestinian perspective, it refuses to give its young readers a simple, single solution. As part of this process older characters keep the younger ones informed about the historical perspective of their struggle and how it extends beyond the foundation of the Israeli state, reaching back to British colonial rule. They also make it clear that Israelis cannot simply be categorised as the enemy. Thus Karim's uncle, recalling his first encounter with Israelis during the 1967 occupation, explains that "'They were bad, good, moral, immoral, some greedy and vain, some kind-hearted and suffering, all just men, women and children – like the rest of us. Human beings.'" (56). These interventions give readers a historical, human perspective on the conflict, and mean that they can create their own interpretation of events by navigating their way through the various voices offered. As children's fiction this is done in a relatively simple way, but it begins to mirror some of the sophisticated multiple perspectives offered by adult literature, including material addressing the Israeli–Palestinian conflict (Khoury 2006).

The activation of multiple voices alerts teachers to the opportunities for creativity offered by certain novels over others. For example, it might lead to a reconsideration of the widespread teaching of such books as *The Boy in the Striped Pyjamas* (Boyne 2006), which centres around a nine-year-old German boy, Bruno, who is so naive that he fails to realise what is going on at the Auschwitz concentration camp, despite living next door to it with his father, the commandant. He meets a Jewish boy, Shmuel, living in the camp on the other side of a barbed-wire fence and they strike up an unlikely friendship. Bruno and Shmuel are identical in age, physical appearance and interests; their only dissimilarity is that one happens to have been born Jewish. In negating differences and not allowing Bruno a historical perspective on what is going on, the conflict in the novel is reduced to the simple matter of good versus evil. Consequently, hearing different voices in the text, be they of individual or broad historical significance, is very difficult. It might be termed a *monologic* novel. As such, I would argue, it limits opportunities for creativity and learning. For while it is much enjoyed and can yield some interesting lessons, it does not offer a variety of responses from its young readers, nor a variety of worldviews from its characters.

Conclusion

The call to pay attention to how texts *sound* is a call to give more thought to the meaning that is contained *within* them. If students are actively and dialogically to engage with texts they need ways of drawing this meaning out. They need the opportunity to grapple with them, experience them as physical objects designed to act upon them, not just be acted upon. 'Reading with the ear', listening to how others read and 'critical listening' all make this possible. They highlight the implied sound carried within all writing and, in many cases, call on students to transform texts by sounding them out loud. Consequently the dialogic nature of language, so keenly discussed in theoretical work, is made real, with the understanding that all dialogue requires a listener, as well as a speaker, made explicit.

Many of the activities in this chapter simply draw attention to processes that are carried out in the mind as a matter of course. We do hear what we read as we process it in our heads. We do read what we hear as we proffer up opinions on everyone and everything. But classrooms need consciously to exploit and extend the commonplace for learning to take place. When students *think* about their reading and their listening additional meaning is created. They are made aware of material in new ways and new material comes into being. If you remain unconvinced, then sit back right now and listen to everything around you: you have just heard something you didn't realise was there.

Key texts

Alexander, J. (2008) 'Listening: The Cinderella profile component of English', *English in Education*, 42(8), 219–233.

Bakhtin, M. (2006) *Speech genres and other late essays*. Austin, TX: University of Texas Press.

Vygotsky, L. (1986) [1936] *Thought and language*. Cambridge, MA and London: MIT Press.

7

Speaking, writing and creativity

Written speech is the most elaborate form of speech.

Lev Vygotsky, *Thought and Language*

While *listening and reading* are receptive processes, *speaking and writing* are generative (Andrews 2010: 72). Rather than being analogous to one another, they share a complementary relationship. Speaking can stimulate writing and vice versa.

Clearly there are differences between the spoken and the written word, evidenced at the most basic level in how easy it is to identify when someone is reading from a script and how difficult it is accurately to transcribe speech (Fowler 1988: 136). The *crafted* nature of a script means that it contains clear linguistic signposts to guide the reader in issues to do with pace and intonation. The *spontaneous* nature of speech and its reliance on paralinguistic features to be fully understood not only makes it difficult to set down in writing, but equally difficult to reproduce as speech once this has been done. At issue for English teachers is whether the disparate functions of language, as exemplified in the difference between a written script and spontaneous speech, make pairing speaking and writing of practical value. Some would think not. For example, Kress (2010) questions the suitability of the word 'language' to encapsulate "the distinct logics of time and space, of sequence and simultaneity" (87) that mark out the "entirely different materiality" of each verbal mode. De Certeau (1988) argues that writing attempts to regulate speech, bringing it within formal limits and so negating the ability of speakers to express themselves and push against accepted norms. Carter (2004), however, offers an alternative perspective, describing how language exists on a "spoken-written continuum". This chapter draws on the idea of a continuum to explore ways in which the creativity of speaking and writing interact and complement one another. This is not to say that they are the same thing, but is to suggest that they share common features, both in the way they are created and how they create. The work of Carter and Bakhtin (2006) is drawn on briefly to illustrate this point, before examples show first how the commonality of speaking and writing can stimulate creativity, and then how each can draw on the distinctive functions of the other.

Links between speaking and writing

Carter (2004), in *Language and Creativity: The art of common talk*, draws on an extensive computerised corpus of spoken language to make the case that "patterns and forms of language which as a student of literature I had readily classified as poetic or literary can be seen to be regularly occurring in everyday conversational exchange" (10). He is not arguing that spoken and written forms are the same but that, in particular uses, they share common features, including ones of creativity. Consequently, when he makes a case for the creativity of 'ordinary' speech, he reaches conclusions that could equally describe the creativity of literary works. He explains that it "engages us intellectually" (10), that "[i]t can prompt thoughts" and "provide new angles on things", that it "can make us laugh at the absurdity of a situation", "enable us to express a critical stance" and "engage us emotionally and affectively". This leads him to determine that "it may be more instructive to see literary and creative uses of language as existing along a cline or continuum rather than as discrete sets of features or as a language-intrinsic or unique 'poetical' register" (66).

The idea of a 'cline', or 'continuum', highlights the links that exist in all language use. Each dialogic exchange creates new meaning and transforms the co-ordinates of a system of language for future use, if only fractionally. Writing, as an advanced, refined form of language, must have developed out of spoken forms and its influence must equally feed back into them. Bakhtin (2006) offers insight into how this process might take shape in explaining how all 'speech genres', be they written or spoken, exist and develop in dialogic relation to one another. He describes how we do not learn a language, but learn how to use language in relation to how others do so:

> Our speech, that is, all our utterances (including creative works), is filled with others' words, varying degrees of otherness or varying degrees of "our-own-ness," varying degrees of awareness and detachment. These words carry with them their own expression, their own evaluative tone, which we assimilate, rework, and re-accentuate.
>
> (89)

Students in today's classrooms have the opportunity to experience this process of assimilation in historically unique ways through exploring the crossover between speech and language in electronic communication. Text-messaging, instant messaging, emailing, online social-networking and blogging, forms that have established themselves on the cultural landscape in only a few years, all tend towards an informal written register that is heavily influenced by spoken forms. This perhaps reflects the fact that they are written with the explicit possibility of an immediate response. They operate as a kind of *speech-as-writing*, a process explored in exercises drawing on the collapse of distinctions between speaking and writing in various electronic media (Box 7.1).

BOX 7.1 Analysing the creativity of *speech-as-writing*

Two of the following tasks draw on forms of digital writing heavily dependent on spoken forms. The third uses an older technology to capture writing *re-created* as speech. All three require learners to reflect on the creative qualities of both written and spoken forms.

1. Analysing an instant-messaging conversation: Students pair off but initially work separately at computer terminals some distance from one another. They begin an online discussion on a topic of the teacher's choice. When this is complete (the teacher sets a clear time limit) the pair come together to analyse what has been written. They consider anything they feel is particularly creative, its similarities and differences to speaking and to more conventional forms of writing, and the consequences of responding in writing within a very limited time period. Topics need selecting carefully for their own generative qualities. Some examples are listed below:

   ■ Discuss a band/ football team/sports star, etc. you both know well.

   ■ Engage in an argument about which is best: sweets or crisps.

   ■ Develop an idea for the perfect holiday.

   ■ Develop an idea for your own reality TV show.

   ■ Discuss which contestant should win a reality TV show you both know well.

   ■ Discuss what developments in technology might occur in the next one hundred years.

2. Comparing blogs and podcasts: Students write a blog on a topic of their choice. For example, they might write a diary-style blog of their day, or the first entry to a blog that will have a specific focus, such as recording their interest in fashion. They then record a podcast on exactly the same topic. Once they have transcribed the podcast, they compare the two with a specific focus on how the written form incorporates elements of speaking and the spoken one elements of writing.

3. Comparing spoken and written narratives: Having read a short story, students record themselves re-telling it. They transcribe at least part of the re-telling and compare it to the original. As with the above task, they comment on similarities and differences between the two. They have a particular focus on techniques used in both written and spoken accounts to hold the reader's or listener's attention.

Differences between speaking and writing

While speaking and writing share common features at various points on the "spoken-written continuum", they also diverge in many ways, particularly in the processes by which they physically come into being. Speech relies on the ability of the mind to use language to process and respond to stimuli at incredible speed. We can name an object the moment we see it and respond to a straightforward question the instant it is asked. In dialogue with others, we can also swiftly move ideas along, each speaker offering a new perspective or new information and so allowing other speakers to offer new responses in turn. This ability to generate additional meanings in response to others, almost at will, might usefully be referred to as a *creativity of proliferation*. It is brought to the fore in *collaborative* (Wells 1986), *exploratory* (Mercer 1995) and *dialogic* (Alexander, R. 2008) forms of talk, which have all been the subject of extensive studies showing how they aid learning. Each focuses on the generative capacity of language in spoken dialogue to advance understanding and bring new meaning into being, not as it is hidden away in the nuances of a word, but as it arises in a whole range of actual spoken statements. In contrast, the creativity of writing, certainly in its more crafted forms, is one of paring down and selecting out. Generativity from such written work stems from the multiple meanings that can come from a particular linguistic construction rather than from literally bringing into being a whole range of stated ideas. Carried out in reflection rather than in a moment, the writer has time to make choices about vocabulary and style. Linguistic creativity in a written text must rely on the relation of words to each other. The text must carry the whole of its sense if readers are going to access it in ways at least vaguely in keeping with an author's intention. In contrast, the creativity of the spoken language can rely on a range of paralinguistic features, including how it is situated within the wider environment. Vygotsky (241) illustrates this using a passage from Dostoyevsky in which six men in conversation use the same expletive in six completely different ways, each making total sense because of the context in which it is used. Readers familiar with the US crime drama *The Wire* might recall similar linguistic creativity in two of the show's detectives sustaining a conversation over several minutes while investigating a shooting using only a single swear word. Spoken language is thus, in many ways, simply a lot easier than written language. But that does not mean that its creativity cannot be encouraged and cannot stimulate learning in particular ways, especially as it draws attention to the connectedness of the social world in which it is used. Boxes 7.2 to 7.4 show how the spoken word can be used to stimulate creativity in preparation for writing tasks.

BOX 7.2 Story-telling in the round

This relies on the capacity to generate imagined worlds from the smallest of stimuli. Working in groups of four or five, one student is given the first line to a story (e.g. The light shone directly in her eyes.). This student must continue telling the story with minimum time for reflection. After thirty seconds or so the story is passed on to the next student and so on. When the story comes to an end, or sufficient time has passed, students reflect on how they were able to keep going. They also consider how the story might have been told differently if written. Finally they write the beginning of a version of the story and reflect on the transformation between spoken and written versions.

BOX 7.3 Verbal tennis

This task stimulates thought and offers an alternative to brain-storming. Students are placed in pairs and told to take opposing sides in an argument. For example, one might be arguing for and one against a proposal to shorten school summer holidays. One student serves by completing the phrase "I think summer holidays should be shorter because . . ." while the other returns with "I think summer holidays are the right length because . . .". They continue back and forth until one player cannot come up with a new response. The task gives students direct experience of articulating words and phrases that can then be used in writing. It also stimulates the creation of new thoughts as students strive to stay in the game and respond to partners.

BOX 7.4 Speaking to a writing frame

Students should have in front of them a frame for a particular type of writing. For example, they might be looking at how to submit a proposal to a toy manufacturer for a new board game. After a few moments thinking to themselves how they might structure a proposal following the frame, they speak it out loud, making sure to include the prompts provided by the teacher. The teacher then removes the frame and asks students to write the proposal themselves. They should have absorbed an idea of the generic conventions required but are also less likely to be rigidly tied to them, as can happen with excessive use of frames.

The creativity that comes from speaking as it prepares for writing does not have to rely on bringing meaning into being in playful ways that involve either quick-thinking or wordplay. It can also rely on carefully organised classroom discussion, either in pairs or small groups, as outlined in Box 7.5.

Speaking can generate meaning quickly and easily because it can draw on all the environmental means at its disposal. If a speaker cannot find the exact word he or she wants, a gesture can be used instead. The respondent can then perhaps provide the word, or they both find a way of understanding without the particular word being needed. Writing does not allow for such luxuries. Thus "we are obliged to use many more words, and to use them more exactly" (Vygotsky 1986 [1936]: 242). Vygotsky argues that as a consequence of writing requiring so much more effort than speaking, it is likely to need working on in order to produce a more satisfactory version. Redrafting he positions as analogous to thinking so that "the evolution from draft to the final copy reflects our mental process" (243). The final written form is not the same as thought, but it is a fuller expression of thought than speech in that it has to include so much more. Thought, existing as the *sense* of inner speech rather than as language itself, contains within it the paralinguistic features upon which speech relies. Thus writing contains a fuller embodiment of a thought than speech. It is harder to think of examples where writing aids the creativity of speaking than the other way around, precisely because of this

---

BOX 7.5 Speaking-to-writing-to-speaking-to-writing

Discussion stimulates thought before writing in offering ideas and perspectives that an individual might not consider on his or her own. These ideas can then be given a fixed form (necessarily selecting from them and generating further meaning) in either individual or group writing. The following activity shows how this stimulation can be ongoing.

1.   A group of four discuss a topic or story idea.
2.   Each member of the group writes a piece of their own informed by the discussion.
3.   The group listen to each other's pieces of writing and discuss what works well and what might be improved.
4.   Individuals redraft their work in the light of the discussion.

Alternatively the group can write together after the initial discussion. They then swap what they have written with another group, which writes comments suggesting what has been done well and what might be improved. The work is returned to groups so they can discuss the comments before redrafting as they see fit.

---

configuration where writing is a more developed form of language use. However, in certain formal speaking situations writing lays a valuable foundation. For example, students should be encouraged wherever possible not to refer to scripts or prompts in speaking activities. Examples such as writing out formal speeches or writing down what might be said in a mock court case help embed patterns of speaking that can be drawn on in actual performance.

While it does not draw on actual speaking, Box 7.6 gives an example of an exercise that encourages students to recognise how complex writing needs to be to convey meaning effectively. The more a completed text is reduced, the less fully it can be understood.

BOX 7.6 Dismantling a text

Ask students to summarise a lengthy piece of writing they have taken some time over in exactly one hundred words. Ask them to discuss with a partner what is lacking in the summary that is present in the original. Direct them to provide information to their partner about what is missing in as complete a way as possible without reading the actual work out. When this is done, ask students to further reduce the work to fifty words. Pairs discuss the difference between the first and second summary. Repeat the process again so that the summary is only ten words long. Finally reduce it to a single word. Ask students to read out the word in a way that it best gets across what they were trying to do in their original piece of writing.

Conclusion

This chapter has not addressed writing in English specifically labelled 'creative', also sometimes referred to as 'original' and 'personal' writing. In a sense, its absence highlights the potential for creativity in all writing. As they bring into being different possibilities for meaning and interpretation, some forms of writing are more creative than others; but the process by which any form, no matter how limited its applications, comes to have its own particular generic conventions is a creative one, indicative of how meaning is constructed in dialogic interaction and so, consequently, always holds within it the potential for change, for further creativity. I like to think of this as the reason literary authors do not refer to themselves as 'creative writers' (Scholes 1985: 12); the term is reserved for those who aspire to full-blown authorial recognition rather than those who have actually attained it. Actual authors are just writers. Yes, they are creative, but not because others are not, or because other forms of writing are not. They are just writers because they are just working (very well) with language in ways that language allows. They are one part of the speaking–writing continuum, but still very much part of it.

Below are summaries of the creativity specific to speaking and to writing. Readers might like to consider how and where they intersect on a continuum in order to consider further their various classroom uses.

Creativity specific to speaking

- Speaking is always in combination with other contextual factors such as gesture, accent, volume and intonation. The combination of all or some of these increases the possibilities for creativity.

- The dialogic interaction involved in speaking is more immediate than that offered by writing, which generally relies on an imagined reader. Everyday talk provokes an immediate response, often creative in the way it builds on, adapts and re-forms what went before.

- Speaking addresses an actual rather than an imagined audience; consequently elements of creativity can be inserted into speech in an instant to try to provoke a desired response.

- Speaking offers the possibility of combining and advancing ideas from a group of speakers rapidly and creatively; all speakers in a group can draw upon each other's resources to reach a conclusion unavailable to an individual (Mercer 1995).

- Speakers can switch rapidly and often between different "speech genres" (Bakhtin 2006) to generate particular effects and advance meaning in new ways.

Creativity specific to writing

- There is a self-consciousness and reflexivity in writing that enables careful consideration to be given to the various creative possibilities available at the moment of composition.

- Writing gives permanence to expression. This allows writers to consider the impact of their creativity on different audiences at different times in different locations.

- Writing can be re-written. In the process of re-drafting new meaning is generated from the original texts. A comparison of different drafts gives direct access to the creativity of composition.

- Writing serves as a readily accessible template for further writing. It can be referred to, borrowed, parodied or pastiched in other texts, thus allowing for creativity beyond its initial embodiment.

- Writing has the potential to create its own audience (while in speaking the audience is already present); thus the creative choices made by a skilled writer bring an audience into being.

Key texts

Bakhtin, M. (2006) *Speech genres and other late essays*. Austin, TX: University of Texas Press.
Carter, R. (2004) *Language and creativity: The art of common talk*. London: Routledge.
Vygotsky, L. (1986) [1936] *Thought and language*. Cambridge, MA and London: The MIT Press.

CHAPTER

8

Critical-creativity

Is there life, for the human imagination, after deconstruction?

Richard Kearney, *The Wake of the Imagination*

Language and letters are not so much a guide to what *is* as a collaborative invention of what *could be*. To move in and out of the wealth of the already written, re-writing, quoting and misquoting as you go, is a profoundly developmental activity.

Ben Knights and Chris Thurgar-Dawson, *Active Reading*

The dominant general sense of criticism is one of fault-finding, with connotations of judgement, especially as applied to the arts and literature (Williams 1983: 85). Judgement, of course, does not have to be negative, though to counter the word's fault-finding implications, positive criticism of the arts and literature is often referred to as "appreciation" (85). Regardless of the tone of response any judgement implies the existence of a norm against which a work is compared. Thus, in a sense, criticism is the antithesis of creativity: it assesses to what extent a text matches or does not match particular standards (including creative ones) and casts judgement accordingly. In this regard it invalidates certain forms of cultural production and restricts rather than encourages an expansion of meaning. It also restricts the possibilities open to young people in forming responses. For if they cannot manipulate the discourse of formal criticism, if they have no understanding of the norm to which they must refer, then they are denied a response to a text. Few teachers would query that part of their role is to teach students this discourse, which, it might be argued, is itself a form of creativity. However, if the subject – not just in its relationship to literature, but to all texts – is to be more than learning (and even playing with) a set form of analysis, then different forms of response need to be made available to students, responses that, in turn, do not limit the creativity upon which criticism might be cast.

This chapter looks at what those responses might be. Using the term *critical-creativity*, it considers why a division between criticality and creativity occurs in the first place before exploring how and why they might usefully be brought together. It draws on Paulo Freire's (1996 [1970]) inspirational work on critical literacy and creativity, adapting his ideas in an attempt to find ways of engaging with texts so as to empower young learners. This involves focusing on critical-creativity as it relates to Freire's ideas about 'reading the word and the world', but it also acknowledges that the world has moved on since Freire wrote, and so borrows from a *design* approach to English (Cope and Kalantzis 2000; Kress 2000), which stresses the importance of students being able to make meaning using the full range of available communication modes. To this end the chapter specifically looks at ways in which students can be given full control of their learning and the forms in which they are able to express it. Examples looked at include a focus on 'whole-text' study, positioning students in the role of the teacher, and using re-drafting to highlight the benefits of seeing learning as a *process*.

A critique of critique

Criticism's historical moment, it might be argued, is past. Kress (2000) calls for a "critique of critique" (160), necessitated by the transition from a period of relative social stability to one of flux and rapid change. In the former, he explains, "critique has the function of introducing a dynamic into the system" (160); it is the means of change, judging cultural and societal forms as satisfactory or otherwise. Creativity in this system is an uncommon event, reserved for an elite few who are able to act on forms in ways unavailable to everyone else. In the latter, in other words the world of today, where representation can draw on the multimodal possibilities of electronic technologies, critique is replaced by "complex orchestration" (160). Individuals are no longer "users of stable systems" but "remakers" and "transformers" of "sets of representational resources". As such the task of textual practice shifts from one of critique to one of *design*; in other words, effective responses in an era of instability do not require judgement but an effective mode of engagement, drawn from one of six elements of design: *linguistic, visual, audio, gestural, spatial* and *multimodal* (Cope and Kalantzis 2000). We show what we think about something by making it in our own image. The criticism – though criticism is not the exact word required – is revealed in what has been created.

This chapter offers a slightly more cautious approach than would be required in embracing *design* fully. It positions *critical-creativity* as bridging the gap between traditional notions of *critique* and those of *design*. On a practical level, this is to recognise the realities of English teachers working within a system that places high value on passing exams requiring a traditional critical approach. However, it also comes from a belief that too much attention to 'design' ignores the receptive nature of much learning (and of much of life in general). For regardless of advances in technology, we still read more than we write, watch more than we film, surf more than we post, download more than we upload and listen to more than we record. *Critical-creativity* acknowledges the creativity of *processing* as well as of *producing*, that learning takes place dialogically in the interaction between the text and the mind as well as in being articulated in a suitable form.

Bringing creativity and criticality together

The risk of a *design* approach is that, in seeking to embrace the liberating potential of new media technologies as representational resources, it pushes aside the reflection so crucial to learning. A continual cycle of making and re-making opens up possibilities for new ways of being and of understanding, but the transformation of source texts must be accompanied by a transformation in thinking if learning is to be advanced. *Critical-creativity* allows for such reflection in offering a transactional approach in which possibilities for critique being creative are set alongside those for creativity being critical.

Unlike traditional forms of critique, then, *critical-creativity* does not operate in general, abstract terms, seeking to pass judgement on cultural production and institute norms; rather it establishes the critical-creative possibilities within all of us, acknowledging that anything we do, anything we create, if it is done from a position of understanding and reflection, is, in its own way, offering a critical comment. In the same way, it recognises the urge and possibility to pass judgement on all aspects of life, but does so with a consideration for the multiple options available and with an understanding that such reflective criticism is a necessary part of developing any textual work. Our way of being in the world is a comment about the world and our comments on the world construct a way of being.

Paulo Freire: critical literacy, creativity and *praxis*

Critical literacy, the practice of understanding the world as it is textually constructed, is not a creativity-friendly term. While Wendy Morgan (1996) devotes an entire book (very persuasively) to outlining how it is "a practice that supplements the rigour of contestation and critique with the play of enactment, the pleasure of embodiment and engagement of the imagination" (205), her limited success in convincing others is perhaps indicated by a joint publication of hers (Misson and Morgan 2006) ten years later, exploring "the limitations of critical literacy in terms of its conceptualisations of significant matters such as individual identity, human emotion, and creativity" (x). Her subsequent book relies heavily on 'the aesthetic' as a way of describing what texts *do* to people and how, in turn, people *do* things to texts. It is this shift to considering the transformational and transactional potential of texts that distinguishes *critical-creativity* from critical literacy. For while proponents of the latter see it as a means to understanding and shaping our subjectivities, by helping us to "actively produce, sustain, and legitimate meaning and experience" (Giroux 1987: 15) and to replace "the authoritative discourse of imposition and recitation with a voice capable of speaking in one's own terms, a voice capable of listening, retelling, and challenging" (20), the start point for this process is critique, *followed by* – though rarely termed – creativity. Implied in the critique is also an unmasking and rejection of the ideological underpinnings of texts; thus any affective, emotional response becomes framed in terms of coercion and manipulation. Consequently the reader is encouraged not to participate in the text but to become distanced from it.

Ironically one of the early inspirations for a pedagogy of critical literacy, Paulo Freire, is at pains to avoid such a separation of critical and creative functions. His most fully developed work, *Pedagogy of the Oppressed* (1996 [1970]), makes reference to creativity, along with related terms such as "transforming", "re-creation", "re-making" and "re-invention" almost as much as it does criticality. Its approach is so useful when considering critical-creativity because it is one of *construction* as well as *deconstruction*; Freire advocates critical awareness as a key step to a complete exis-tence by linking it to the process of creative transformation (29). In other words, he does not offer a critique in order then to create, but develops a theory that does both simultaneously. In doing so he develops his own distinctive terminology, outlined below to give a fuller picture of how his ideas might translate to the con-temporary classroom.

Key concepts in Freire's idea of *praxis*

Banking versus problem-posing education

A *banking* system of education involves knowledge being transmitted, in limited form, from those with power to those without. It does this in the anticipation of a passive, uncritical reception, with no prospect for dialogic engagement or chal-lenge. A *problem-posing* education seeks to challenge all knowledge and in doing so to transform it. It involves active, critical, dialogic engagement, starting from the perspective of what the learner wants to know, not what he or she ought to know. When Freire writes that "[b]anking education inhibits creativity" (64) while "[p]roblem-posing education bases itself on creativity" (64), he draws attention to how one system seeks to fix existing constructs in place, denying new configura-tions of meaning to develop from below, while the other "affirms men and women as beings in the process of *becoming*" (64); in other words constantly involved in bringing meaning to their own worlds and in doing so transforming the social world at large.

Reading the word and reading the world

Freire does not see human potential as being realised simply through learning to read, but through learning to read critically. This, he explains, involves reading 'the world' as well as 'the word'. We must bring meaning to the world by naming it; the world, in turn, is transformed by this process, constantly named afresh in acts of "creation and re-creation" (70). The whole process is dialogic as contesting versions of the world come into contact so that "once named, the world in its turn reappears to the namers as a problem and requires of them a new *naming*" (69). This idea clearly links to those of situated learning, stressing the importance of context and drawing on prior experience in order to exploit the transformative capacities of language.

Action-reflection and *praxis*

Praxis is used by Freire to signify the coming together of *creative transformation* and *critical inquiry*. The former is seen as a process of actively working on material, in this case language, the latter one of thinking about it. He sees the two as inseparable, coming together in what he also calls *action-reflection*. He explains that 'the word' carries within it the potential for both *reflection* and *action*. This involves coming to an understanding of language within one's own social existence and of the possibilities for its use. It is the logical consequence of a *problem-posing* approach to education that seeks to challenge and transform knowledge. Critical reflection upon 'the word' – thinking about how and why this challenge might come about – leads to the creative action of 'the word', as its transformed use generates alternative meanings to challenge conventional ways of being. In this model, which stresses the dialogic nature of language as it both acts on and is acted upon by users, "to speak a true word is to transform the world" (68).

In his articulation of *action-reflection* and *praxis* Freire wants learners not just to understand the world, but also to change it; in the understanding comes change. He develops his ideas as part of a radical programme for fundamental reform of the structures of society in his native Brazil. This book has more modest aims for its more modest times, which is why it favours a term such as *critical-creativity*. It doesn't for a moment want to suggest that the situation of English school students today is similar to that of Brazilian peasants in 1970. However, it does want to suggest that different classroom approaches can result in profoundly different outcomes, if not of how the world operates then of how it is perceived, and of the kind of learning that takes place within it. This necessitates a shift away from linking outcomes in the classroom primarily to the accumulation of various skills and to examination success (though both, I would argue, need not and should not be sacrificed); instead, it requires English teachers to have more lofty aims, to draw on some of the optimism of Freire's not so long ago days, so that they can conceive of helping students become "more fully human" (26). For it is surely within the compass of the subject to raise critical awareness and, simultaneously, to enable the creative transformation of an individual's environment as part of ". . . the drive to search, the restlessness, and the creative power which characterize life" (42).

P.E.E.: limiting criticality and creativity

The pressure to achieve examination success and to teach to measurable targets within the space of a single lesson has led to some peculiarly uncritical and uncreative practices in English. In my regular observations of subject trainees, a significant number of lessons refer to a technique for structuring writing called P.E.E., which stands for Point – Evidence – Explanation. It is used extensively in helping students compose non-fiction texts, such as argumentative pieces, and in textual analysis. Students make a point, back it up with evidence and then explain the evidence. A simple P.E.E. paragraph (the three sentences required of the technique are nearly always elevated to the status of a paragraph) might look like this:

> Dickens uses lots of rhetorical devices at the start of *Bleak House*. For example, he repeats phrases about fog many times. This is to stress the dark, grim, secretive nature of London at the time when he was writing.

There is nothing inherently wrong with such work. It provides students with a safe, comforting frame within which to develop an essay. What is too often lacking in lessons that use P.E.E., though, is any acknowledgement of an alternative. For example, the same 'paragraph' might be evidenced and explained as follows:

> The constant repetition of the word "fog" in the opening of Dickens's *Bleak House* gives a rhetorical emphasis to the dark, grim and secretive nature of London at the time when he was writing.

The differences are minor. However, the reduction of three sentences into one is not simply a technical advance. There is a unity to the thought process that goes into such a sentence, a sense that the impact of the repetition can be *felt* in the course of reading rather than reduced to a formulaic interpretation. It is the fog that is important, not the search for a rhetorical device, nor the effort then to explain that device.

It could be argued that the technical competence required to write the second example is not available to less able students, so justifying the focus on P.E.E. for a considerable number. However, it does little more than provide a single way of engaging with a formal discourse of criticality. Consequently it risks becoming a hollow frame into which students can transpose any point that the teacher wants them to make in order to prove that a particular learning objective has been met. The example just given is the type of response likely to be produced in a lesson with the objective of learning about the use of repetition as a rhetorical device. Once such an objective is established and students are told to identify repetition all they need do is mechanically complete the P.E.E. format. The content becomes irrelevant. For example, the focus could have been shifted to descriptive language with the following written:

> Dickens uses lots of detailed description at the start of *Bleak House*. For example, he mentions that the smoke filling the air has "flakes of soot in it as big as full-grown snowflakes". This emphasises the grim environment of London at the time when he was writing as human pollution has taken over from nature.

Such techniques belong to an education of memorisation rather then learning, of banking received knowledge rather than asking questions of it. Even the example that strays from the P.E.E. model limits meaning to what can be explored within a conventional critical discourse. Placing such restrictions on responses is frustrating when it is relatively straightforward to see how very simple forms of engagement with *Bleak House* that start with personal responses can generate a far greater range of meanings. For example, any of the following might be used:

- Explain why you do or don't like the opening to *Bleak House*.
- Write to Dickens as a literary editor telling him why you think his use of the word "fog" is either inspirational or tedious.
- Storyboard the opening sequence to a television production of *Bleak House*. Write the script for a narrative voiceover to accompany the images.
- In pairs develop a reading of the opening section for an audiobook. The audio version is to be abridged, so you must first halve the length of the opening, but without losing its core meaning.

These may seem like small points with which to start an exploration of the practical application of critical-creativity, but without such activities there is the risk that students do not learn from texts in terms of discovering and generating meaning from and for themselves; instead texts serve as repositories of obscure information and linguistic features, to be extracted as directed.

Critical-creativity and wholeness

To Freire, creativity is an act of humanity, part of a drive to bring about the "'humanization' of the oppressed" (26). Such a claim seems remote from the reality of teaching the language of advertising to Year 9 on a Friday afternoon. However, it is linked to giving people the potential to understand the world and their place in it as fully as possible, so that they might live as full an existence as possible. This is not done in the sense that individuals can ever be 'complete', filled to the brim with whatever potential they possess, but that they can learn to use critical and creative skills to understand the continual state of 'becoming' in which they live. Key to this is giving them full access to the material of their existence and presenting it to them in a way that encourages exploration rather than simple acceptance. P.E.E., used excessively and at the cost of alternative approaches, is an example of how certain practices can be limiting. It denies other forms of response and only allows for exploration of particular elements of a text. If English is to play its own small role in the quest for a fuller humanity, then the least it can do is offer students full, meaningful access to the material of study. As the next section shows, this can be done in very simple ways, such as making sure that they can study whole texts, rather than fragments, and that texts are explored for what they mean rather than as repositories of linguistic features.

Newspaper work: from a skills-based to a critical-creative approach

In searching for material linked to young people's lives, teachers are adept at selecting newspaper articles to use as models: human-interest stories, celebrity gossip, sports reports, etc. Generally they are used to stimulate writing an actual article. This is invariably to record information about a topic unrelated to the news article itself, for example, reporting on an incident in a novel or writing up a school event. As such, the content of the stimulus material, while chosen carefully, is rarely a feature of learning. It simply offers a template for some of the generic structural conventions of newspaper articles: *how to write a headline, how to position a by-line, the 5Ws, writing a caption, how to set out a quotation*, etc. The argument here is that even when the content of an article is unrelated to what students go on to write about, it is the content that offers a template for further writing as much as structural features.

While it is useful for students to be reminded of the structure of any written form, often the majority already recognise the features to which they are directed. They have probably experienced this lesson many times in their school lives, not just in English, but also in other subjects that use newspaper articles as a way to explore ideas. Such teaching is a good example of the well-intentioned, but ultimately de-motivating, focus by teachers on skills at the expense of content, on words and sentences as opposed to the whole text. Ironically students are presented with material of real interest but rarely get the chance to engage with it – either critically or creatively.

A critical-creative approach recognises the need for a full understanding of what we read in order to write from a model without simply copying it, to re-create rather than re-produce. Vygotsky (1986 [1936]) describes writing as the process which gives the most direct access to thought. While thought condenses language, reducing complex patterns to a single word, writing, in order to be understood by the reader, must be expressed in full. Thus students' minds, in order to understand and practise how to write a newspaper article, have far more to gain from looking at a whole text and its *content* than from endlessly analysing headlines and opening sentences. Their minds need the opportunity to reduce a whole text to a single thought (or a few thoughts) if they are to develop an understanding of how it works and produce a similar one of their own. This cannot happen with a predominantly skills-based approach that constantly offers up disembodied words and phrases for analysis, thus reducing the generic conventions of a text to a list of rules to be replicated. The generic conventions of newspaper articles – and of nearly all texts – are much more various and fluid than the simple positioning of structural devices. For example, they involve gradations of tone, bias, and levels of formality and must consider audience and the particular newspaper being written for. Consideration of such key elements requires engagement not simply with the mechanics of a text but with its creativity, with its own process of 'becoming' and, in turn, with its criticality, with how it takes its place in the world.

It would seem a tall order to teach all of the above if simply using an article as a model so that students themselves can write one as part of work not actually related to newspaper study. However, the example that follows draws on the idea that a whole text can be stored in the mind as *sense*, its complex structures and details understood without necessarily having to be broken down into constituent parts. It draws on a *critical-creativity*, in seeing textual construction as being reliant predominantly on meaning as it is situated within a whole text and suggests that if students are allowed to engage critically with the whole then they are more able to have the creative capacity to produce whole texts of their own in response.

To reflect the fact that teachers often select articles from newspapers published on the day of teaching, the story below (Figure 8.1) is from the *Daily Mirror* on the day this section of the book was written. It is likely to stir responses either of

ATTACKING FROM REAR

MoD tells girls: boozing makes you fat

EXCLUSIVE

BY CHRIS HUGHES
SECURITY CORRESPONDENT
c.hughes@mirror.co.uk

WOMEN soldiers are being warned to drink responsibly by the Ministry of Defence... or they will end up with big bottoms.

Chiefs have resorted to the shock tactic to stop thousands of women in the forces from binge-drinking.

The MoD produced the hard-hitting advert after discovering that increasing numbers of beer-swilling service-women are running a health risk.

Adverts in Soldier magazine feature the slogan "Does My Bum Look Big in This?" against a pint glass made to look like a woman with a large bottom. It asks: "Are You Drinking to Excess?"

A forces insider said: "We are determined to show there is no place for excess drinking in the British Army and shock tactics are a great way to

DOES MY BUM LOOK BIG IN THIS?

ARE YOU DRINKING TO EXCESS?

▲ **BOTTOM LINE** Powerful MoD advert

get the message across to both men and women."

The campaign comes after a recent MoD-funded survey which showed as many as 23,000 members of the armed

forces – around one in seven – were drinking "hazardous and harmful" levels of alcohol.

The study also showed those who have served in Iraq or Afghanistan are 22% more likely to develop serious drink problems than other troops.

There are around 18,000 women in the forces, making up 9% of the total of the UK's service personnel.

Binge-drinking is defined as having six or more units of alcohol on one occasion on at least a weekly basis.

The MoD said it took the issue of problem drinking very seriously and stressed the consumption of alcohol was strictly regulated when personnel are serving on operations.

Last year the MoD launched similar ads in Soldier magazine, featuring the slogan "Lager, Lager, LARGER!" in a bid to stop male soldiers binge-drinking.

One showed a pint glass made to look like a bloated torso with a bulging tummy and droopy man boobs and also asked: "Are you drinking to excess?"

FIGURE 8.1 'Attacking from rear', *Daily Mirror*, 12 January 2011

amusement or mild offence, and so readily engage students in a move towards critical engagement, creative interpretation and an awareness of the various possibilities available when writing themselves.

Newspaper analysis often starts with the headline. A skills-based approach in this case would direct attention to the pun contained in "Attacking from the rear". It may not, however, explore the implications of the language. A pun has been used: that is all you need to know. The next task is often to spot the '5Ws' (who, what, why, where, when) in the first sentence. This article is not ideal for such work. After all, it only reliably provides the reader with who and what. Yet this is the most appropriate model to be found in this particular edition of the paper. Newspapers themselves, it seems, rarely follow the conventions expected in the classroom. And even if the conventions are in place, what about the content? Are women really being warned against drinking by the MoD so that they do not get big bottoms? And what about the rest of the article? Where is the space to consider the hard-hitting facts in the second half? Somehow the article warrants doing more with it than simply breaking down its component parts. Yet it is difficult to envisage an alternative approach that does not clumsily direct students to see the underlying ideology constructing gender and identity in the piece.

A solution rests in a critical-creativity that gives students time to absorb the *whole* article with no direction towards any specific components, before encouraging them to act on the text in a way that allows for a variety of responses. This could be staged as follows:

1. Reading time: students read the whole article themselves with no specific instructions. They reduce the article to three words to replicate Vygotsky's model of storing complex ideas as sense.

2. Forming an opinion: still on their own, students write a short paragraph advocating one of the following standpoints:

   a. This article is informative and fun at the same time.
   b. This article is offensive to women.

3. Discussing an opinion: students compare what they have written in groups of four. Each group concludes whether or not it approves of the article and pens a collaborative response to one of the statements in point 2.

4. Close reading: each group writes an additional paragraph, drawing on the whole text to back up its opinion. They are not simply looking at the functional purpose of the language used (e.g. 'attacking from the rear' is a pun to catch the readers' attention), but at the different ways it can be interpreted within that function (e.g. the pun in the title is meant to be funny, but is also sexist, trying to get a laugh out of female soldiers charging at the enemy with big bottoms).

This approach may prove difficult for less able students and so requires careful planning. However, allowing students to absorb the impact of what an article says gives them the chance to consider often overlooked elements such as tone, bias, formality and audience. It encourages a sophistication of response and the possibility of different responses, preparing students for their own writing in a way that moves beyond the simple physical structure of the text on the page.

When I showed this text to a class almost all felt it was fun rather than sexist. They felt it got across a serious message and that the reference to "girls" rather than women in the title simply reflects a common way of speaking. I challenged their opinions, suggesting that the editorial decision to use the article in the first place suggests a particular way of constructing women. Armed with their own readings they were able to resist my objections. *Critical-creativity*, however, develops as more information becomes available, accepting that a text can act on its readers in different ways at different times as more information becomes available. Readers might like to consider how their own opinion is modified after reading the following article (Figure 8.2), which appears on the same page as 'Attacking from Rear'.

Model soldier ready for war

SHE'S patrolled the catwalks as Miss England, but soldier Katrina Hodge faces a new mission, in Afghanistan.

The 24-year-old, dubbed Combat Barbie, has returned to the Army after her model stint and could now be sent to war. Katrina, of Brighton, said: "Coming back was a culture shock."

FIGURE 8.2 'Model soldier ready for war', *Daily Mirror*, 12 January 2011

Students as teachers: critical-creativity and role-play

Role-play in young children is conventionally viewed as a rehearsal for real life. In playing at 'Mummy' and 'Daddy', children are preparing to take on these roles in adulthood. At secondary level children no longer engage in such activity spontaneously. When they do use role-play in lessons there is little sense of preparation for adulthood; rather it is used to develop ideas on an area of study, be it in examining a fictional character, or preparing points of argument for a debate. Described like this, the purpose of role-play at different stages of development appears to be radically different. In young children it is a naturally occurring phenomenon, fundamental to building an understanding of the world, while in early and late adolescence it is a technique for expanding knowledge. However, it is possible to look at role-play in a way that finds common ground in how it is used at different ages, one that links it to a notion of creativity as a core human attribute, rather than an adjunct to the rest of life.

To develop a theory of role-play and creativity, it is useful to view taking on roles as a safe, acceptable way of challenging conventional norms, of, to return to the work of developmental psychoanalyst, D. W. Winnicott (1971), being 'non-compliant'. Winnicott positions creativity as a universal human quality manifested in our relationship with external reality (67). Looking primarily at the play of very young children, he suggests that

> the creative impulse is . . . something that can be looked at as a thing in itself . . . something that is present when *anyone* – baby, child, adolescent, adult, old man or woman – looks in a healthy way at anything or does anything deliberately . . ..
>
> (69)

This rather vague statement risks over-generalising what is meant by creativity. However, it is made in the context of observations that see experimenting with and taking on various roles as fundamental to cognitive development. For these activities expand the cognitive domain and allow humans not to accept the world as a given. Exploration is not just of a specific role, but of *difference*. Role-play in this sense is not a rehearsal for adult life, it is part of life itself, and to limit its use is to limit learning. In Winnicott's terms it is even to limit a fulfilled existence. For creativity can be seen as the instinct to push against accepted norms, to experiment with perceptions of the world. He offers what he admits is an overly-simplified dichotomy to stress his point, arguing that "living creatively is a healthy state, and that compliance is a sick basis for society" (65).

Winnicott's words offer a particular challenge to schools, which operate in a system where non-compliance is anathema. Role-play can offer a safe environment in which to challenge this state of affairs. It offers experimental ways of not fitting in, of rebelling and trying out new options. As such the creative positions taken up by students offer a critical engagement with texts, challenging them to formulate responses beyond the remit of the norms expected of them when not in role.

In a sense all schools privilege compliance over creativity, if not in their stated aims, then in the structures they reproduce. Regardless of whether or not an institution engages in progressive pedagogical practices, students are just that: students. As such they take on the social and cultural baggage of their role: in the ways they respond to learning, in their relationships with teachers, in their attitudes to each other. They are at school to learn and they learn *from* their teachers. This problematises any attempts to structure learning so that it starts with the knowledge and interests of students. Within the construct of traditional teacher and student roles, that starting point tends to develop towards the knowledge base of the teacher, rather than expanding on the initial offerings of the students. Anecdotally this might manifest itself in students demanding to know what a piece of writing means despite having already explored it and themselves given it meaning. There is a reluctance to accept, and so develop further, their own understanding, given it is their role to learn from the teacher. This is not in any way intended to undervalue the potential input of teachers, but to suggest that significant learning can come from challenging rather than complying with accepted wisdoms: this involves students developing a greater sense of the value of their own ideas. Paradoxically, this might best be achieved by enabling students to express those ideas in the guise of another. One way of doing this, a practice increasingly used in schools, is to place young people in the role of the teacher, encouraging small groups to teach the rest of the class. The obvious rationale for doing this is that it forces students to look closely at material and that, in teaching something, they remember it more effectively. Winnicott's ideas about creativity, however, allow for a more radical view: approaching material as teachers rather than students changes the nature of that material itself. It also changes the thought structures placed upon that material and so extends the argument for such an approach advancing learning. In becoming teachers young people are forced to 'non-comply' with their established ways of thinking. They leave behind the passive construct of the student, with the various positions this offers different individuals depending on their particular circumstances and levels of motivation, and take on the dynamic, interrogative approach of the teacher. In their actions they become at once critical and creative.

Re-drafting as a critical-creative process

Vygotsky (1986 [1936]) tells us "written speech is the most elaborate form of speech" (242). This, he explains, is because it lacks the "situational and expressive supports" of verbal communication, such as gestures and tone of voice. Meaning "must be achieved only through words and their combinations", resulting in "complicated forms" that often require re-drafting. In this re-drafting, I would like to suggest, the action-reflection of the critical-creative process is laid bare: the *creative-action* of the re-write comes about through *critical-reflection* on the original, giving those with access to all drafts involved insight into the writer's "mental process".

There is an assumption in the above that all writing is creative. This is clearly not the case. Much teaching seeks to impose particular conventions on young writers in order to induct them into the functional use of particular 'text types', with the result that "millions of notebooks, examination papers and essays are crammed with words, which are in essence no more than transcriptions, the forced labour of submission" (Rosen 1992: 127). Of the three dominant approaches to the teaching of writing, *process-based*, *genre-based* and *skills-based* (Robinson and Ellis 2000), it might be argued that only the first overtly encourages creativity. The latter two, often linked closely together, risk ignoring the creativity of a whole text's construction, instead focusing on its component parts and neglecting the subtle choices involved in actual writing (though this need not be the case with a *genre-based* approach, as suggested in exploring the newspaper article above). A *process-based* approach, meanwhile, "theorises writing as a recursive, cognitive process" (72), thus encouraging a transactional response to writing as words are simultaneously brought into being and reflected upon.

The examples in Boxes 8.1 to 8.3 draw on re-drafting as a means of ensuring critical-creativity in a range of activities. Each requires students to reflect upon the process of writing, to consider what has already been written in order to bring about changes, be it in physical configuration or meaning. As such, each stresses the need for a *critical-creative* approach to ensure that the impetus for students' writing comes from their own minds even when drawing on models and ideas offered by teachers.

BOX 8.1 Using models for redrafts

Genre-based approaches to writing often rely on models. Students are given an example of a particular genre and asked to replicate it. This risks a "loss of creativity on the child's part and a subordination of the child's creative abilities to the demands of the genre" (Kress 1982: 11). One way to limit this subordination is to direct students to write a first draft in the style of a particular genre without a model. Most secondary students will be familiar, if not expert, with a range of genres and capable of doing this. It forces them to engage with their own 'mental processes'. Only when a first draft is complete should students be exposed to a model. In comparing this to their own work they can plan for any adjustments needed to fit the requirements of a genre. The second draft is likely to fit more than the first with dominant norms, something that students should reach for if they are to have control of their writing, but the route to this 'compliance' is creative, enabling students to reflect on and understand how they need to adapt their writing in order to fit within a particular pattern.

BOX 8.2 Studying how others redraft

Wilfred Owen's 'Anthem for Doomed Youth' is perhaps the most famous example of redrafting available for study. Examining how, in collaboration with Siegfried Sassoon, he develops various drafts (available in full at the Oxford University First World War Digital Poetry Archive, www.oucs.ox.ac. uk/ww1lit/) shows the 'mental processes' of poets at work and allows students to reflect on how this might apply to their own writing.

Only the first four lines of two versions are reproduced here in the interests of brevity, but the whole poem can be used for the following activities. They are designed to enable critical-creative engagement with the drafts, while allowing students to reflect on how they might use redrafting with their own work.

1st draft

Anthem for Dead Youth

What passing bells for those who die in herds?
Only the iron anger of the guns.
Only the shattering rifles rattled words
Can patter out your hasty orisons.

Final draft

Anthem for Doomed Youth

What passing bells for those who die as cattle?
Only the monstrous anger of the guns.
Only the stuttering rifles' rapid rattle
Can patter out your hasty orisons.

1. Give the first draft to a small group. Ask them, in role as First World War poets, to change three parts of the poem without taking away its core meaning. They can change a single word or a whole line. Question them, still in role, on whether or not they think the changes are an improvement. Finish by giving them the final draft and asking them to consider the changes made by Owen in comparison to their own.

2. In role as Owen and Sassoon, pairs discuss the first draft. The student playing Owen articulates what he was trying to do when writing; the one playing Sassoon explains what the poem means to him. Both then begin to work on possible improvements.

3. Hold a press conference in which Owen and Sassoon are questioned about changes to the drafts. If possible display both prominently in the classroom so that those in role can draw attention to various sections.

4. Ask students to pair up and work on redrafting a piece of work together. At the end ask them to reflect on how having another person making suggestions about their work affected the final draft.

BOX 8.3 Redrafting according to set instructions

The difference between *creative* and *re-creative*, or *transformative*, writing is that the former stems from the imagination while the latter relies on a source text to respond to or change into something else (Knights and Thurgar-Dawson 2006: 104). Re-creative writing lends itself to critical-creativity because it offers students the opportunity to reflect on differ-ences between the original and any transformations. Creative writing has only itself as a reference point and so is more difficult to reflect upon. Reflection, as shown above, can come from comparing drafts, but at times changes might be relatively small and so comment limited. One way to overcome this is to design activities that require students to redraft work radically. The three suggestions below do not necessarily make for better writing, but generate alternative texts and enable reflection on the writing process.

1. Random changes. Give students a series of random changes to make to a text:

   ■ replace all words beginning with 'b' with words starting with 'g';
   ■ give all characters new names;
   ■ add three adjectives;
   ■ remove five words.

2. Shortening drafts:

   ■ Direct students to write a piece of work to a specific length within a time limit.
   ■ Ask them to re-write the work so that it fits a reduced word count, again within a time limit. Lead them to think this will be the final draft of this piece.

> - ■ Ask for a further prescribed reduction in length.
> - ■ Compare various drafts and reflect critically on the process.
>
> 3. Combining writing and other modes of design:
>
>   - ■ Show students a visual adaptation of a written text.
>   - ■ Ask them to write a short piece based on what they have seen.
>   - ■ Look at the original written text and compare it to their own work.
>   - ■ Re-draft their own writing in the light of what they have learned from both the original and its visual adaptation.

Conclusion

The majority of the examples in this chapter focus on the use of writing in critical-creativity. This is not to deny the possibilities opened up by other modes of *design* as discussed in its opening paragraphs. They are multiple and should be extensively drawn on by teachers both to stimulate students and further learning. The prevalence of written activities, however, reflects the centrality of 'the word' in *critical-creativity*, not just as it is read or transcribed on the page, but as it works to process activity in the mind, to bring thought into being (Vygotsky 1986 [1936]: 218). *Critical-creativity*, it might be said, is forged in the mind, as prior knowledge and new material is reflected and acted upon in order to create something new. Attention can be drawn to its transactional nature in making the following points:

- ■ Anything we write we also read.
- ■ Anything we read we also write, be this literally or in the way we process it internally.
- ■ Anything we write we have the capacity to re-write.
- ■ Anything we read we have the option of reading again in a different way.
- ■ Any criticism we make is created within a particular context, or role.
- ■ Any creativity we exercise has the potential to offer a critical comment in the choices it makes within a particular design grammar.
- ■ Writing is one of several options available to us in fixing meaning in time and space. Part of the critical engagement with response comes in deciding on the mode of fixing meaning.

Censure of the material offered here might come from teachers – rightly – concerned about the necessity of preparing students for formal assessments that still, by and large, rely on students commenting on writing using traditional forms of criticism. There is no way of avoiding directing students to engage with material in this way and to write within the formal discourse of literary criticism. That discourse, however, always needs filling with content. Even in a system obsessed with final exams, I would argue, *critical-creativity* provides innovative, stimulating and cognitively challenging ways to generate such content. It allows students a playful, experimental, even rebellious approach to learning that can be re-formulated to the compliance demanded of formal assessment as and when necessary.

Key texts

Freire, P. (1996) [1970] *Pedagogy of the oppressed*, trans. by M. Bergman Ramos. London: Penguin.

Kress, G. (2000) 'Design and transformation: New theories of meaning' in B. Cope and M. Kalantzis (eds), *Multiliteracies: Literacy learning and the design of social futures*. London: Routledge, pp. 153–161.

Misson, R. and Morgan, W. (2006) *Critical literacy and the aesthetic: Transforming the English classroom*. Urbana, IL: NCTE.

9

Creativity and culture

Creative activity, reflection and expression are in all young people's lives all of the time – only they have different names.

Paul Willis, *Common Culture*

. . . the complexity of the idea of culture is nowhere more graphically demonstrated than in the fact that its most eminent theorist in post-war Britain, Raymond Williams, defines it at various times to mean a standard of perfection, a habit of mind, the arts, general intellectual development, a whole way of life, a signifying system, a structure of feeling, the interrelation of elements in a way of life, and everything from economic production to political institutions.

Terry Eagleton, *The Idea of Culture*

The meaning of 'culture', arguably one of the two or three most complex words in the English language (Eagleton 2000: 1), evolves hand in hand with that of 'creativity'. Their symbiotic relationship, in which creativity brings culture into being and culture stimulates further creativity, remains stable, even as the terms themselves undergo radical transformation. So when creativity is conceived of as lying in the hands of an elite corps of artistic geniuses, then culture refers to the creative output of such men (and occasionally women). When creativity is repositioned as a resource upon which all people can draw to shape their own subjectivities and bring meaning to the world, then culture correspondingly expands beyond its elitist horizons, referring both to general ways of life and to the many forms of symbolic representation operating in such lives.

The limitations of the first approach to creativity are obvious. Any attempts to fix culture as lying within a limited canon of artistic production require an acceptance rather than a questioning of value. Learners can interpret this culture but only within the narrow remit of 'appreciation'. Creativity is given to them through the culture of others and cannot be developed further. The contemporary alternative brings its own problems. For when creativity is a process of continual making and re-making and culture has no fixed referent points, then subjects dealing with culture, such as English, may lack direction in establishing the content for study. And any content that is laid down by national curricula or examination boards is open to challenge and rejection by its users, even as they are forced to engage with it.

The reality of English as practised in schools is that its content still carries considerable traces of an older approach in which culture is fixed. For example, canonical texts still dominate examination syllabuses and the teaching of Shakespeare in England is compulsory across a range of age groups. At the same time pedagogical approaches stress the need to draw on the prior knowledge and experience of students in order to bring their own cultures into the classroom. One attempt to reconcile this seeming contradiction has been the development of a range of active approaches to literature, perhaps best exemplified in Rex Gibson's (1990) work on teaching Shakespeare. In demonstrating how students can bring their own creativity to traditional texts, such work is invaluable in helping maintain interest and motivation. However, it perhaps offers too one-sided a perspective on the relationship between culture and creativity. In stressing the creativity that young people can actively bring *to* culture, it risks ignoring the creativity that exists *in* culture (though clearly Gibson himself feels this creativity is there). For if the subject is still to include a canon of work in an era that recognises the limitations of a canonical approach, then it needs to develop a contemporary theory of why certain texts matter. It needs a way of recognising the creativity of those texts, and their cultural 'value', if they are not to appear simply as arbitrary choices upon which to focus work or, perhaps worse still, as the outmoded relics of a traditional establishment clinging on to the last vestiges of a cultural imperialism.

This chapter seeks to find approaches to English that reconcile the creativity young people can exercise in generating and claiming cultures of their own with the creativity of the cultures presented to them in the classroom. It readily accepts the futility of attempting to fix culture, but also makes a claim for the persistence of certain cultural forms, albeit as they are constantly given new shape and expression. In doing so, it draws first on the work of Raymond Williams (1958a, 1958b, 1961, 1977, 1983), which offers a useful bridge between the two polarised models of creativity and culture set out above, seeing how this in turn can combine with more recent ideas about *multiculturalism* and *idioculture*. It then explores a range of examples of teaching creativity and culture, with a focus first on the transformation of cultures, with an emphasis on shifts across boundaries of ethnicity and history, and second, on the creativity of cultures of production.

The creativity of a common culture

In a pioneering rallying-cry, now over half a century old, Williams (1958b) proclaims that "culture is ordinary". He means two things by this. First, that culture is everywhere and exists in the ordinary activities and interactions of everyday life; second, that culture, as represented by particular forms of artistic expression, is not an elite pursuit, but something available for the use of all. Drawing on seemingly irreconcilable Marxist and Leavisite traditions, he explains that culture "is always both traditional and creative" (11), thus establishing an approach that enables people to create their own cultural meaning from the material of their lives while also drawing on the creativity of a more stable, established culture. Showing remarkable prescience he anticipates developments in school English (as, for example, shown in Chapter 1 when discussing Dixon's (1967) *Growth through English*) by almost a decade in linking both elements of culture to *experience*, explaining that "[t]o take a meaning from experience, and to try to make it active, is in fact our process of growth" (1958a: 338). Experience lies both in personal interaction with everyday life and in what we take from texts: it is created and it is received. Thus his prescience extends into developing a theory of culture and creativity with implications of self-construction within the remit of the culture we are given, as demonstrated further when he writes that "[s]ome of these experiences we receive and re-create" (338) while "others we must make for ourselves, and try to communicate" (338).

The phrase Williams uses to describe the cultural mix that results from these processes of reception, re-creativity and communication might make contemporary practitioners wary of fully embracing his ideas. For he advocates the promotion of a "common culture" (337), a term seemingly at odds with contemporary notions about topics such as *multiculturalism*, *difference* and *hybridity*. Further investigation into what exactly Williams means by this, however, reveals ideas that stress the commonality of creative *processes* by which culture is constructed, rather than to actual cultural *content*. He admits that in general terms culture discriminates rather than unifies, finding a particular path for a particular interest or way of being, so that "in its whole process, [it] is a selection, and emphasis, a particular tending" (337). However, he goes on to explain that

> [t]he distinction of a culture in common is that the selection is freely and commonly made and re-made. The tending is a common process, based on common decision, which then, within itself, comprehends the actual variations of life and growth.
>
> (337)

Commonality in this construction does not equate to consensus and conformity, but to constant development, contestation and adaptation. In a system in which culture is persistently worked upon and re-created, particular forms emerge that offer some stability and continuity, but always with the possibility of change.

Williams is not just ahead of his own time. A fellow Marxist cultural theorist claims many years later that "we have yet to catch up with [his position]" (Eagleton 2000: 122). When another, Paul Willis (1990), uses the phrase 'common culture', he positions it in opposition to 'high art'. While he makes interesting points about bringing the "symbolic creativity" of young people's lives into the classroom, so that it "transforms what is provided and helps produce specific forms of human identity and capacity" (111), he does not take on board Williams's point that the separation of culture, be it into categories dictated by age, social class, artistic value, ethnicity or anything else, renders ideas of commonality redundant. Willis's approach privileges youth culture over other forms. Thus any cultural form categorised as 'high art' is there to be transformed into something relevant and usable to a youth identity. Absolutely this should be one of the aims of English practitioners addressing culture and creativity. But consideration also needs to be given to the creativity of *all* cultural forms and how it might work on those who receive it. In other words, it needs to consider the persistence of writers such as Shakespeare and explore whether this has, indeed, anything to do with the specific creative qualities of his work. For the creativity of a 'common culture', in Williams's terms, works not just on the popular cultural products of the everyday, but brings meaning to – and simultaneously is affected by – material from outside one's own realm of experience.

From a common culture to multiculturalism

Multiculturalism refers to situations in which a range of cultures exists side-by-side. Predominantly, culture in this instance refers to ethnicity. Thus in conurbations in the United Kingdom, multiculturalism might involve groups originating from around the world, with different interests, faiths, histories and expectations, living in close proximity. Put like this, the term seems innocuous enough. It is, after all, descriptive of actual conditions in many towns and cities not just in the United Kingdom, but also across the world. And in the interplay of these various cultures, presumably possibilities for creativity exist, in the cross-fertilisation of ideas and the opportunity to draw on a wide range of different ways of seeing the world. The term, however, is currently often used in a pejorative sense by both the political right and left. The right sees the promotion of multiculturalism as at the expense of the core values that they believe lie at the heart of a national society. It encourages particular ethnic groups to make claims for their own identity interests, thus preventing any collective idea of a society based upon a shared national culture. The left has similar reservations about "the rise of identity politics, corporate multiculture and an imploded, narcissistic obsession with the minutiae of ethnicity" (Gilroy 2002: xiv). This is not because of a wariness of multiculturalism *per se*, but a reaction to its uncritical use in encouraging a separation and self-interest that denies the complexity of how identities are constructed and the possibilities for human development in borrowing and adapting rather than simply preserving and resisting. Any narratives of group identity necessarily omit points of difference and contestation. And no culture can preserve exactly some kind of core identity situated in the midst of so many alternative ways of being. Consequently, in an attempt to reclaim multiculturalism, "[w]e should view human cultures as constant creations, re-creations, and negotiations of imaginary boundaries" (Benhabib 2002: 8) in which we are all constantly engaged in a dialogue with ourselves and with others in negotiating the terms of our identity and the world in which we live (16). In doing this multiculturalism builds on rather than rejects ideas of a 'common culture'; multiculturalism is an inescapable part of all our identities and drawing on rather than resisting its many diverse strands helps us understand "the actual variations of life and growth" (Williams 1958a: 337).

Multiculturalism and idioculture

Multiculturalism is an unavoidable state of being for anyone wishing to develop an idea of culture that embraces the whole of his or her existence. To resist it is to limit creativity; to embrace it is to stimulate creative possibilities. These possibilities are enhanced if the concept is widened to account for differences not just in ethnicity, but also in all aspects of social life, for example, in age, gender, specific interests, social class, etc. This is not to denigrate the importance of ethnicity in forging cultural identity, but to suggest that it is but one part, no matter how important, and so must not be promoted at the exclusion of others. To do so would be to exclude possibilities for creativity and learning. For if learning, in part, comes from understanding and drawing on the context of our existence, then we must strive fully to open ourselves up to all of that existence.

Multiculturalism, put like this, is too vast and complex to understand in its entirety, a concept with the potential to cover everything. However, teachers can direct students to draw on the resources of multi-culture in particular ways. A starting point is to consider their own unique cultural configuration, what Attridge (2004) calls an "idioculture". The term refers to

> the way an individual's grasp on the world is mediated by a changing array of interlocking, overlapping, and often contradictory cultural systems absorbed in the course of his or her previous experience, a complex matrix of habits, cognitive models, representations, beliefs, expectations, prejudices, and preferences that operate intellectually, emotionally, and physically to produce a sense of at least relative continuity, coherence, and significance out of the manifold events of human living.
>
> (21)

An idioculture, put like this, is not innate, nor does it stand still. Thus teachers can seek a role in its development in directing learners to reflect on their own experiences in particular ways and in exposing them to new ones.

What has all this to do with English and creativity?

The opening paragraph of this chapter explains the symbiotic nature of the relationship between creativity and culture: as creativity brings culture into being so culture stimulates further creativity. Much of the subsequent focus has been on the different forms of culture available for English practitioners, culminating in a reconfiguration of 'multiculturalism' to take into account the entire complex array of forces at play in the world, a unique combination of which act upon the individual in the formation of an 'idioculture'. It is perhaps also useful to consider the different forms of creativity that track cultural diversity. For it is not just the stuff of cultural representation that marks out difference, but the way it is brought into being. For English, this might mean a particular focus on the different configurations of language used in different forms, or on the preference of one mode over another; perhaps it lies in the particular medium of cultural production, or in whether the creator strives for originality or re-creation. These points have all, to some extent, been explored in previous chapters. For each has covered various elements of the 'culture' of English. It makes it difficult to differentiate examples in this chapter from the rest of the book. The examples that follow might well fit easily into other chapters, but have been selected for use here either because they belong to emergent cultures of which young people are in the vanguard, or because they combine elements of more than one culture.

Transforming cultures

It is possible to talk of Shakespeare and transforming cultures in several ways. His work transforms the cultural worlds of an audience and an audience transforms his work as it creates its own version. Additionally his work is transformed over time according to the historical context in which it is performed and, as it spreads globally, it is also transformed by geographical context. In its persistently iconic status as a benchmark for the quality of literary writing, it makes for an interesting study of the *memetic* (Dawkins 1989 [1976]) process by which culture is passed on across generations. The example here explores using a *Manga* version of Shakespeare in the classroom, identifying four broad patterns of cultural transformation upon which teachers and learners can draw: the transformation of *modal culture*, of *medial culture*, of *social culture* and of *historical culture*.

Using Manga Shakespeare

Teachers are adept at using film and other media to teach Shakespeare's plays, primarily to further comprehension. Difficulties in understanding the language can be overcome when words are put into action (obviously the point of the plays in the first place). The language is easier to understand when combined with images not just because the latter *show* the action, but because the words become *situated*.

Each new version – or transformation – of a play situates its language in a different context, thus creating different connotations in the interplay of the verbal and the visual. It is possible that the more imaginative the transformation of context, the more learning can be stimulated, as new and memorable connections are made between the original script and its transformed setting. In a sense a play is transformed each time it is performed, but the word is used here to refer specifically to occasions when the original text is re-created in modes and media not originally intended.

Graphic novel adaptations are particularly rich in transformative potential, primarily because the dominant *mode* shifts from the linguistic to the visual, but also because the *medium* moves from playscript to comic with all the particular *social* connotations the latter brings and, potentially at least, the setting can be in a new *historical* period. In broad cultural terms the transformations represent a move from high culture to popular culture: the new text is not just created in different ways but has different creative connotations.

The creativity of adaptations can be extended by the imaginative extension of cultural boundaries within credible limits. Early efforts at putting Shakespeare in graphic form show that creativity can be limited if this is not the case and the text is translated into pictures that draw on conventional codes of what Shakespearean characters and settings look like. The first series of graphic novels to re-create classic texts is a case in point: *Classics Illustrated*, published in the United States from the 1940s to the 1970s, follows a fairly generic formula, which suggests that the comics are primarily for educational purposes, providing an accessible route into difficult texts (Versaci 2007: 186). Increasingly, however, transformations combine many of the strengths of graphic novels with the power of Shakespeare's plays, generating versions largely faithful to the original that also offer something entirely new, "exploit[ing] the fact that comics can, visually, take the reader anywhere" (198). For example, Oscar Grillo's re-creation of *The Tempest* (2009), which describes the artist as 'director', sees the play transcribed in its entirety alongside highly original comic images that highlight the fantastical elements of the play (see Figure 9.1). Given the fantastical element of Shakespeare's original, though, the force of this graphic version relies solely on *modal* and *medial* transformations. Several of the plays are also now available in a *Manga Shakespeare* series, which also transform their social and historical directions. A close examination of a Manga version of *Macbeth* (Deas 2008) demonstrates the *cultural creativity* involved in its production and in the way it can be read. The following four analyses draw on a single image (Figure 9.2).

Modal transformation in *Manga Macbeth*

Visual modes offers a more immediate, visceral form of engagement than written ones. In the case of still images, particularly when placed in sequence, the reader has the option of skimming over them quickly, or of taking time to look closely at each. He or she also has the option of reading them in non-chronological order and of re-viewing images at leisure. Such a re-viewing might involve trying to notice something different that is in front of the eyes. This, in turn, involves actively thinking about the connotations of an image as it links to others and to experience in general. The corporeal and the cerebral are drawn on simultaneously. Re-reading takes place much more within the mind. Thus graphic novels offer young people a different modal culture to written text. In one sense their accessibility might encourage connotations of enjoyment and fun; in another of something being easier. The importance of both is all too often overlooked in the classroom. It also places an intimidating piece of high culture within a culture of accessibility and familiarity.

A switch to the visual does not mean that the text does not require active engagement in order to generate meaning. It simply possesses a creativity that is different to the written. For a single image can be loaded with meaning and

FIGURE 9.1 Cover of Oscar Grillo's illustrated version of *The Tempest* (2009)

FIGURE 9.2 Page from Robert Deas's *Manga Shakespeare: Macbeth* (2008)

connotations, both as it stands alone and as it relates to the rest of the text and the world beyond. In Figure 9.2 the eye is drawn to the dominant image of Macbeth in the lower frame. The frame at the top is initially passed over. Without accompanying text it is unclear what is happening. The eye might take in the target centred on King Duncan's face, but needs to look at the frame below to understand fully why it is there and to understand why the frame is bordered in black in a particular shape. Reading Macbeth's first thought bubble requires the reader to recall what has been happening in the play so far. Evidently he is thinking about killing Duncan, and so the target becomes clear, as does the reason for its appearance. He is holding a pair of binoculars, the shape of the upper frame. The two frames can now be connected. The gap between them – the "gutter" (McCloud 1994) – holds implied rather than openly stated meaning. Here this meaning is relatively straightforward to fill in. Macbeth has been looking through the binoculars at the figures below him. The target on Duncan's face represents the possibility of killing him. Macbeth is contemplating whether to do it or not. Reader and character alike are given the opportunity for contemplative repose in the graphic novel form.

The reader may well pass over both images in a moment. However, they can still be returned to. They contain within them meaning that stretches beyond the mere instant referred to in the play. Macbeth's gaze holds within it all the inner turmoil and indecision he is experiencing at this point. Lady Macbeth's stare, directed at Duncan, indicates her own desire to see him dead. Banquo's equally stern gaze, despite his wearing an eye-patch, suggests he is an oppositional force to this desire being fulfilled without complications.

Of course, other readers might construct meaning from the frames differently, but they are likely to follow a similar pattern given the conventions of the graphic novel genre and the *Macbeth* plotline. The creativity comes from constructing the images in such a way that they contain so much meaning pertaining to the whole of the play.

Medial transformation in *Manga Macbeth*

If we are concerned to bring the experience of young people into the classroom then it is important to offer access to familiar media. The graphic novel form will not play a role in the lives of all students, but the links it has to 'youth culture' and to exploring often fantastical issues beyond the possibilities of everyday life extend the potential meaning to be drawn from Shakespeare. Suddenly he can be positioned as a counter-cultural force, engaged in moving beyond societal boundaries and norms.

Social transformation in *Manga Macbeth*

The most striking feature of a Manga version of Shakespeare lies in how it transforms characters into a world of Japanese-inspired action heroes and villains. The clear division of good and evil emphasises the confrontational nature of the

Macbeth storyline. In Figure 9.2 clearly all the characters are engaged in struggle and conflict. While Macbeth occupies most space, Duncan, particularly as he is targeted, is broad of shoulder, suggesting he occupies a (threatened) position of authority. Meanwhile, the sharp hairpin emerging from the back of Lady Macbeth's head gives her an aggressive quality reflecting her own social transgression within this male-dominated world.

Historical transformation in *Manga Macbeth*

This particular version is removed from an obvious historical context. The costumes suggest a future world, but it is clearly post-apocalyptic, as shown by the modern buildings in a state of collapse (also suggestive of earthquakes, given the Japanese style). The use of binoculars clearly removes the action from Shakespeare's time. In framing the top image through the binocular lens, the artist is inviting the readers to consider what it is like to contemplate Shakespeare's plays through an alternative time-frame.

The above all focus on the experience of *cultural transformation*. Those unconvinced of its efficacy might like to look closely at a graphic version of *Pride and Prejudice* (Petrus and Butler 2010) (Figure 9.3), which remains faithful to Jane Austen's storyline as well as the social and historical setting, but draws on elements of high romance, women's magazines and chick-lit in its design, presenting a whole new range of connections from which the learner can draw. Such transformations demonstrate the creative possibilities within which producers of culture can work. They offer a starting point for teachers to consider how to direct students to create transformations of their own that aid learning about particular texts but also about the generation of cultural meaning itself.

The creativity of emerging cultures: gaming lessons for the non-gaming teacher

James Paul Gee's *What Video Games Have to Teach Us About Learning and Literacy* (2007), concludes that "We have no idea yet how people 'read' video games, what meanings they make from them" (218). They would appear, then, to have little place in an English classroom concerned with how meaning is generated; what use is something that cannot be read, that cannot have meaning extracted from it, in a subject all about meaning? A focus on culture and creativity, however, allows for reflection on how a form of representation develops, how it takes its place in individual or group life. It does not need to be 'read', as in understood, but can be looked upon as a particular component within an existence: what can be 'read' is how the representation fits into a life, into its world of use, rather than what it specifically has to *say*. Consequently, video games are an interesting medium to explore regardless of a teacher's own level of competence, by asking the question: *what is gaming culture?*

FIGURE 9.3 Cover of Hugo Petrus and Nancy Butler's illustrated version of *Pride and Prejudice* (2010)

The following activities require students to bring their own knowledge of video games to the classroom in order to explore and explain themselves how video games can help people to learn. Bringing together the cultures of the classroom and of gaming enables a fresh perspective on both. Before starting the work, it is worth discussing with students whether some kinds of games have more potential than others to advance learning. For example, Gee argues that the most effective are those in which players take on particular roles and identities, or in which they build and develop complex entities, such as cities, armies or social networks.

Activity 1: teaching video games

Video games involving role-play offer players transformative experiences, as they step into an alternative identity or even build up an identity themselves. The activities proposed here are analogous to such a gaming process in encouraging students to take on the role of teachers in educating their classmates about a particular game. Thus they transform their classroom identities in exploring a medium all about transformation. The same principles of transgressing social norms outlined in the use of students-as-teachers in Chapter 8 apply here, although on different terms. Here the students begin as the experts. The transformation is as much of material as of selves. By engaging with their own 'symbolic creativity' from a new standpoint they can consider more fully its cultural implications.

Teachers need to decide the level of input they offer based on the ability and confidence of students. Most effective is an approach that encourages participants to envisage how video games themselves stimulate learning. Groups struggling to generate their own ideas can be given a pared down list of some of Gee's own (216–217). For example he identifies "some of the reasons why good video games engage players with powerful forms of learning" as being that:

- they offer players strong identities;
- they encourage players to think like scientists;
- they position players as producers rather than consumers;
- they make failure acceptable;
- they encourage creative solutions to difficult problems.

A difficulty in teaching any of the above lies in groups having material for the rest of the class to work on. Interactive whiteboards can help, but where unavailable, learners can still give a presentation on how the game of their choice stimulates learning.

Activity 2: defending gaming

Presenting arguments for or against an issue is an activity much used in English. To make it more stimulating, small groups should decide in what form they want to make their case defending gaming. For example, they can use a traditional speech, perhaps aimed at a group of concerned parents, or they can make a short video presentation. To mirror and parody the sensationalist discourse that exists against gaming, students can be encouraged to make grand claims about the learning opportunities presented, perhaps using a title such as 'Why gaming teaches me more than school' or 'Why gaming makes young people the geniuses they are today'.

Activity 3: the design grammar of gaming

"Video gaming," Gee tells us, "is a multimodal literacy *par excellence*" (18). A focus on gaming should encourage students to develop their own theories about the 'design grammar of gaming'. They can learn about how meaning is created through looking for patterns in the six areas of design (Cope and Kalantzis 2000): *linguistic, visual, auditory, gestural, spatial* and *multimodal*. Games incorporate all elements, often in interesting ways for learning. For example, when words do appear on the screen, they absolutely serve a purpose and disappear once this is done. They are a very good example of a *situated* literacy, devoid of meaning without their particular context (218).

Activity 4: developing games

Students draw on ideas they have developed about a design grammar to inform planning a game of their own. Focus should be given to the kinds of learning promoted by the game. What kind of thinking do players need to engage in to progress further? What kind of identities do they take on and how does this offer new experiences? What worlds or identities do players need to construct as they are playing? What kind of creative thinking will help them overcome challenges?

Teaching any of the ideas above requires students to have confidence in what they are doing. Without strong guidance they may not be able to bring their knowledge about gaming to classrooms in ways that will genuinely stimulate learning. Students without such knowledge will also need engaging in other activities. The potential for a meaningful exploration of culture and creativity, however, is clearly present. The next step for teachers keen to pay more than lip-service to the idea of bringing young people's own experiences into the classroom is to engage with software that allows students to develop actual games.

Traditional text as hypertext

Shifting from a world in which text is principally read on the page, be it in books, newspapers or magazines, to one in which it is as likely to be read on a screen offers opportunities for creativity in exploring the cultural transformation that takes place in the transference from one to the other. A story written in a book is not the same story when reproduced on a screen. In part this is because of the physicality of reading, different connotations arising from the materiality of a book compared to a screen, but it is also because of the different cultural connotations attached to both forms. There is no escape from a book, particularly a straightforward chronological narrative. The reader must press on, one word, one page at a time, if he or she is to find out more. Consequently it can hold connotations of difficulty and effort, requiring a long time to finish, with the ultimate reward unclear. For confident readers it can also connote security and comfort, demanding total immersion and so exclusion from the irritations of everyday life. A screen, in the shape of a website, does offer escape. Hyperlinks embedded in a text can literally transport the reader to another place. The reader can also cut and paste sections at will, working on them, re-creating them to his or her liking. There is not the same requirement to stick with a text to the end, or to be subservient to its demands. Consequently it can have connotations of fun, or experimentation, and of the reader being in control of the material. These respective connotations can be drawn on not just in reading texts in different media, but in re-creating one text in another format. The example in Box 9.1 looks at re-creating a book as a website.

BOX 9.1 From text to hypertext

This example uses Joe Simpson's (1988) *Touching the Void*, an account of his survival after a mountaineering accident in the Andes. Unusually for a work of non-fiction, it now appears on exam syllabuses, which itself poses interesting questions about the status and creativity of different literary forms. The task requires students to create a website exploring the multiple issues and themes that arise from the book. On completion of the website (though, of course, a website can always be added to and so might never be deemed complete), students reflect on the meaning it generates compared to the book as a form of cultural representation. The website also serves the purpose of setting down a narrative and the many thoughts associated with it in a non-narrative form. Thus the website will not necessarily contain text from the book, but will have a range of links for further exploration. In a sense the website is analogous (in an organised way) to the thoughts a mind might hold about a book. It raises key questions about the experience of a book in terms of its content and information compared to the way it is written and structured. These are some of the words and phrases that might be hyper-linked in this example: *Peru, Simon Yates, the movie, Joe Simpson, famous tales of survival, books about mountains, films about mountains, the world's most dangerous mountains, climbing equipment, the Andes, climbing terms, famous mountaineers.*

Conclusion

Applicants for places on the postgraduate teaching course I run at London Metropolitan University are asked the following question at interview: *How should an English department in a school with a diverse multicultural and multilingual intake approach its curriculum?* There tend to be three types of answer offered. The first focuses exclusively on the 'multilingual' aspect of the question, talking about the need to support EAL (English as an Additional Language) learners and to make material accessible. This response scores low in the selection process, failing to spot opportunities offered by the cultural and linguistic diversity students bring to the classroom. The second type of response talks about finding out about the cultural backgrounds of the students and adapting material accordingly. This scores more highly, suggesting awareness of how to draw on students' own knowledge in learning. The third relatively rare response is the one received most favourably. It acknowledges the impossibility of finding source material that reflects the culture of all students and so, instead, suggests an exploration of the diversity of texts in general. This involves both drawing on the backgrounds of students and teaching texts from a range of sources, with the focus of learning on neither, but on the opportunities offered by diversity itself.

Were I to engage in discussion with interviewees rather than push them out of my office after their allotted fifteen minutes, I would chat about the nature of diversity itself. For currently the word is used almost exclusively, like multiculturalism, to refer to ethnicity. Absolutely this is a key element of cultural difference and the interplay of different forms of representation that can be borrowed from around the globe is a rich source of creativity and learning. However, too narrow a focus on a single element of diversity, be it to do with ethnicity or otherwise, risks limiting classroom opportunities. It calls for meaning to be fixed rather than explored and to exist in isolation, as belonging only to a particular group, rather than shared and adapted with others. It also risks essentialising particular groups, affording the same qualities to a whole range of individuals, and so ignoring the 'idioculture' of each. This chapter has deliberately steered clear of linking culture – and also multiculturalism – too much to ethnicity. It sees culture as existing in all the elements of life, so necessitating an approach that values difference not for itself, but for its part in the creation of a social whole. Again, this is not a fixed whole, but one ever-evolving in a process of contestation and negotiation, a 'common culture' of process rather than content.

It strikes me that the final example used above, involving the transformation of a narrative account into a website, might seem too removed from general discussions of culture to belong to this chapter. However, it has been included deliberately to draw attention to how the terms of culture never stand still. For in a little over a decade contemporary culture has come to focus as much on the means of production as on what is produced. Meaning is now created not just through choices in consumption but through choices in *how* to consume and, in turn, how to re-create. Where once we simply watched, listened and read, now we also film, upload and hyperlink. Such developments can be intimidating for teachers, particularly those not very familiar with digital technologies. Much of this book has been keen to stress that new communicational modes need not overwhelm and replace more traditional notions of the subject entirely. However, they cannot be ignored, both because they are so integral to the lives of so many young people, but also because they have such potential in promoting creativity and learning. Half a century after Williams proclaimed that "culture is ordinary" it is time to update him and declare too that "creativity is ordinary". It has always been so in the inner resources of the mind, able to project a range of readings onto a range of material, but now we all have the potential to choose to express this creativity in forms previously only dreamed of.

Key texts

Attridge, D. (2004) *The singularity of literature*. London: Routledge.
Williams, R. (1958) *Culture and society*. London: Hogarth Press.
Willis, P. (1990) *Common culture: Symbolic work at play in the everyday cultures of the young*. Milton Keynes: Open University Press.

Conclusion

Creativity and *not* learning

> The question 'What is *learning*?' implicitly raises the question 'What is *not learning*?'
>
> Gunther Kress, *Multimodality*

There is a contradiction at work in promoting creativity within an education system that pays a great deal of attention to 'standards'. In English schools the word is generally applied in two ways. Most common to teachers is its application to a particular level of attainment at a particular age. Thus the 'standard' to be reached by the age of fourteen is a 'level 5' in English, Maths and Science. Its use in the media and the wider population is more likely to apply to 'standards' of behaviour, which are invariably 'falling'. Both indicate a value attached to norms of behaviour and performance and suggest the undesirability of deviating from them. Creativity has no real value or relevance in such a system because the teacher's focus is on directing students to learn, behave and perform in set ways that are passed down from above, rather than encouraging them to explore a range of alternatives in order to build on their existing knowledge. This is obviously a relatively simplistic model of learning as it occurs on the ground, ignoring the agency that remains with individual teachers, the to and fro of everyday class-room life, and even the inclusion of creativity within curricula, as has happened in England, both in English as a discrete subject and as a cross–curricular focus (QCDA 2007). However, it does raise interesting questions about what happens when students step outside prescribed parameters and engage in *not learning*, a term borrowed from Gunther Kress (2010) to describe the learning that occurs beyond official definitions of the term. He explains that "'*not learning*' refers to the same processes and phenomena as *learning*, though outside of institutional framings and their metrics" (179). In being removed from official frameworks of learning they come instead to be "called *experience, development, meaning-making* and so on", all terms that are closely linked to creativity in this book.

This final chapter casts an irreverent glance at what might pass for *not learning* in English. It calls on teachers to seek occasions when students can do what they are not supposed to do because in some ways that is how creativity and learning work. Both require moving beyond accepted and established patterns to bring new meaning and knowledge into being. Learning cannot simply reproduce what is out there in the world; it needs in some ways to transform it. And this means young people sometimes challenging what teachers are supposed to teach and how they are supposed to teach it. As a product of the late twentieth and early twenty-first centuries rather than the 1960s and 1970s, my call for action stops short of handing learning over entirely to students, but it asks teachers to think carefully about some of the practices that are often uncritically pushed in schools today.

What follows is not based on theory, research or academic reading, but on my own growing sense that variety and experimentation is being drummed out of the profession, not because of a lack of skilled practitioners, but because of demands placed upon them. The practices I call on to be challenged are not inherently damaging in themselves and I have used all of them in my own teaching many times over. So please don't feel bad if you recognise yourself in what I write. But they become damaging if used excessively and at the expense of other ways of doing things. If teaching replicates the same methods continuously then how can learning occur? Where is the transformation of our knowledge base? What is the point of education at all?

Assessment for *not learning*

In the rush to meet demands that formative assessment occurs in every lesson there is a danger that attention is paid to the act of assessment rather than its purpose. For example students are often asked to self-evaluate their work but in doing so are invariably drawn back to an objective they were given at the start of the lesson. As well as taking up a large chunk of lesson time, the process becomes self-fulfilling, students knowing they were supposed to learn, for example, about how camera angles in film have particular connotations of meaning and so commenting that they learned that camera angles in film have particular connotations of meaning. I'm being slightly facetious, in that there is the possibility for self-reflection in such a process. However, cognitive engagement with a task might be increased if students are not so conscious of providing a response that will please the teacher. Instead, they can be encouraged to comment on what they have *not learned*: on ways in which meaning is generated other than from camera angles. This is likely to produce a range of responses and reveal the many different processes at work in film and the viewing process.

Not learning objectives

Focusing on a particular objective at the start of a lesson dictates in very limiting ways the parameters for the learning that can take place. If the objective is not met then learning has not taken place, regardless of what else has gone on in the lesson. Objectives, looked at like this, are as much tools for measuring teacher effectiveness

as for moving on learning. An alternative calls on the creativity of students to identify *not learning* objectives they have met. They can do this by writing an alternative
learning objective that they think could have been used at the start of the lesson.

Not a plenary

The dangers of an excessive focus on formative assessment and learning objectives
combine in the form of a plenary, a short section at the end of lessons to recap on
previous learning or to introduce a new element of learning. Nothing, it seems
to me, has encouraged a transmission style of education more than the plenary, a
space where students are led to tell teachers what they want to hear, be it in
confirming they have met objectives, or assessing the level to which the objective
has been met. Creativity can be brought to this process by focusing on transformation rather than transmission. Students, for example, can be encouraged to
(knowingly) give the wrong response. Perhaps they can write a small piece in an
incorrect register, or using a particular linguistic effect to excess. They can offer a
parody of a response, exaggerating what is expected of them, or giving it in deliberately misleading terms.

Not literature

Students can be encouraged to bring in texts from home that they think will
definitely not be on English exam lists, e.g. comics, magazines, genre fiction. They
should explore these texts using the terms they have met in 'literary' study, or,
alternatively, argue as to why they are of more 'literary' merit than a particular text
that is on the curriculum.

Not a text type

Alongside studying a standard text type, such as writing to persuade, students can
be encouraged to re-create the work in an inappropriate form, e.g. using the
language of romantic fiction in a persuasive speech. If this proves difficult, students
are usually capable of transforming almost any text into language that draws on
their own vernacular.

Not correctness

In order to encourage writing and a free-flow of ideas, it is often useful to stress to
students that they can write for a period of time without worrying about accu-
racy. This works well when using a 'stream of consciousness' style of writing to
generate thoughts for further work. Students are asked to write continuously about

whatever is in their heads and to try to keep their pen going at all times. From time to time the teacher can intervene to ask students to write about something specific.

Not describing

Teachers can challenge the common misconception that descriptive writing requires lots of rhetorical flourishes by calling for redrafting that relies on 'description by omission'. In other words, first drafts are stripped back to reveal the effect of a more sparing approach to style and vocabulary. Revisions depend on the work that students have produced, but in the first instance might require them to remove three adjectives. They could then be called upon to only use 'said' as a verb describing speech. They might then have to reduce the length of the piece overall by ten words. Finally they might have to remove any remaining adverbs. This task works particularly well on word-processing programmes, where texts can be altered very quickly. The process can also be carried out on an actual piece of text for study, students working on re-creating it according to instructions. The finished product may not be a particularly 'good' piece of writing, but the process of transformation will draw attention to particular effects of language.

Not vocabulary

Teachers should resist the temptation to provide vocabulary lists to help with understanding of texts. The meaning of a word will only emerge in context and so students need the opportunity to work out what they think a word means themselves before being provided with an official definition, if one is still required. Students should also be encouraged to accept that they can easily understand long pieces of writing without knowing what every word means, thus removing some of the anxiety many feel about being able to comprehend complex texts. They can also be encouraged to replace words they do not know with ones that they do, even if they are not absolutely sure it maintains the general sense of a text.

Not writing

Teachers need to accept that some commonly taught forms of writing are no longer in general use outside the classroom. Writing to instruct, for example, is becoming increasingly redundant as a form. New technologies, such as smart-phones, generally do not provide instruction manuals. Users must intuitively work their way round a device and seek help online if necessary. Online advice may well come in the form of a short instructional video, invariably available on Youtube. Teachers can exploit this shift to explore the possibilities of different modes that are *not* writing. For example, students can be directed to make instructional videos of their own. This, in turn, allows them to reflect upon the purpose and function of different modes of communication and to question the dominance of writing in the classroom.

Not reading

Teachers should arrange a library lesson and deliberately use it to show a short film. This is then used to inform a discussion about the relative learning qualities of reading and viewing. This should not be done didactically with the intention of persuading learners to the merits of one medium or the other, but to draw very specific attention to the different processes at work in each. Additionally it raises issues about libraries as sources of information. How much, for example, do people rely on books for information – or even for reading for pleasure – rather than other media?

Absolutely the role of schools is *not* to create *not* students for a *not* society. They are very much part of society and key to how young people are inducted into all our shared futures. We need to consider carefully, though, what is meant by sharing. Are learners to share in the same experiences? Or are they to share their own experiences with other learners? The distinction is important. For the first model promotes a vision of society where harmony comes through conformity, while in the second it is achieved through difference. The latter is the model very much favoured here. The former discriminates and divides, allowing only certain ways of being to be valued and to be fully expressed. The latter takes all values and forms of expression into consideration and strives not to discriminate. It is a model that sees creativity and learning as analogous to one another, democratic processes that are central to shaping our *individual* identities, but also our *shared* identities. For when creativity and learning are viewed like this it allows everyone to share in creating and learning from the social world, as each identity acts on and in that world.

The focus on *not* learning offers a gentle rebuke to some of the dominant discourses at work in schools. These tend towards notions of control, conformity, standardisation and compliance, so offering a model of sharing values and methods imposed from above. Creativity never simply accepts what is given; nor does learning. Both involve a transformation of the self and of the world in a process that, as Freire says, "makes possible the pursuit of a fuller humanity" (1996 [1970]: 29).

References

Alexander, J. (2007) 'The uncreating word: Some ways not to teach English', in V. Ellis, C. Fox and B. Street, *Rethinking English in schools*. London and New York: Continuum.

Alexander, J. (2008) 'Listening: The Cinderella profile component of English', *English in Education*, 42(8), 219–233.

Alexander, R. (2008) *Towards dialogic teaching: Rethinking classroom talk*. York: Dialogos.

Almond, D. (1998) *Skellig*. London: Hodder Children's Books.

Almond, D. (2010) *My name is Mina*. London: Hodder Children's Books.

Andrews, R. (2001) *Teaching and learning English: A guide to recent research and its applications*. London and New York: Continuum.

Andrews, R. (2010) *Re-framing literacy: Teaching and learning in English and the language arts*. London and New York: Routledge.

Apple, M.W. (2004) *Ideology and curriculum*. London and New York: RoutledgeFalmer.

Appleyard, J.A. (1994) *Becoming a reader: The experience of fiction from childhood to adulthood*. Cambridge: Cambridge University Press.

Arizpe, E. and Styles, M. (2003) *Children reading pictures: Interpreting visual texts*. London and New York: RoutledgeFalmer.

Armstrong, I. (2000) *The radical aesthetic*. Oxford: Blackwell Publishers.

Arnold, M. (1971) [1869] *Culture and anarchy*. Cambridge: Cambridge University Press.

Attridge, D. (2004) *The singularity of literature*. London and New York: Routledge.

Bakhtin, M. (2006) *Speech genres and other late essays*. Austin, TX: University of Texas Press.

Baldick, C. (1983) *The social mission of English criticism 1848–1932*. Oxford: Clarendon Press.

Banaji, S. and Burn, A. (2008) *The rhetorics of creativity: A literature review*. London: Arts Council England.

Barnes, D. (1976) *From communication to curriculum*. London: Penguin.

Barnes, D., Britton, J. and Rosen, H. (1969) *Language, the learner and the school*. London: Penguin.

Barthes, R. (1977) *Image/Music/Text*. London: Fontana.

Beghetto, R.A. and Kaufman, J.C. (eds) (2010) *Nurturing creativity in the classroom*. New York: Cambridge University Press.

Belbin, D. (2011) 'What is Young Adult Fiction?', *English in Education*, 45(2), 132–145.

Benhabib, S. (2002) *The claims of culture: Equality and diversity in the global era*, Princeton, NJ and Oxford: Princeton University Press.

Blackmore, S. (1999) *The meme machine*. Oxford: Oxford University Press.

Bok, C. (2008) *Eunoia*. Edinburgh: Canongate.

Boyne, J. (2006) *The boy in the striped pyjamas*. Oxford: David Fickling Books.

Brindley, S. (ed.) (1994) *Teaching English*. London and New York: Routledge.

Britton, J. (1993) [1970] *Language and learning: The importance of speech in children's development*, 2nd ed. Portsmouth, NH: Boynton/Cook.

Browne, A. (1981) *Hansel and Gretel*. London: Walker Books.

Browne, A. (2011) *Me and you*. London: Picture Corgi Books.

Browne, E. (1994) *Handa's surprise*. London: Walker Books.

Bruner, J. (1986) *Actual minds, possible worlds*. Cambridge, MA: Harvard University Press.

Bullock, A. (1975) *A language for life*. London: HMSO.

Caldwell Cook, H. (1919) *The play way: An essay in educational method*. New York: Frederick A. Stokes Co.

Calvino, I. (1982) *If on a winter's night a traveller*. London: Picador.

Carter, A. (1981) *The bloody chamber and other stories*. London: Penguin.

Carter, R. (2004) *Language and creativity: The art of common talk*. London and New York: Routledge.

Cassidy, A. (2005) *Looking for JJ*. London: Point.

Child, L. (2008) *Goldilocks and the three bears*. London: Puffin.

Clarke, S., Dickinson, P. and Westbrook, J. (2009) *The complete guide to becoming an English teacher*. London: Paul Chapman.

Cliff Hodges, G., Moss, J. and Shreeve, A. (2000) 'The future of English', *English in Education* 34(1), 1–11.

Cope, B. and Kalantzis, M. (1993) *The powers of literacy: A genre approach to teaching writing*. Pittsburgh, PA: University of Pittsburgh Press.

Cope, B. and Kalantzis, M. (eds) (2000) *Multiliteracies: Literacy learning and the design of social futures*. London and New York: Routledge.

Craft, A. (2005) *Creativity in schools: Tensions and dilemmas*. London and New York: RoutledgeFalmer.

Craft, A., Jeffrey, B. and Leibling, M. (2001) *Creativity in education*. London and New York: Continuum.

Cremin, T. (2009) *Teaching English creatively*. London and New York: Routledge.

Culler, J. (1975) *Structuralist poetics: Structuralism, linguistics and the study of literature*. London: Routledge & Kegan Paul.

Culler, J. (1982) *Deconstruction: Theory and criticism after structuralism*. London: Routledge & Kegan Paul.

Damasio, A.R. (2000) *Descartes' error: Emotion, reason and the human brain*. New York: Quill HarperCollins.

Davison, J. and Dowson, J. (eds) (2009) *Learning to teach English in the secondary school*. London and New York: Routledge.

Davison, J. and Moss, J. (2000) *Issues in English teaching*. London and New York: Routledge.

Dawkins, R. (1989) [1976] *The selfish gene*. Oxford: Oxford University Press.

Dean, G. and Barton, G. (eds) (2011) 'The future of English: One subject, many voices', *EnglishDramaMedia*, 20, 29.

Deas, R. (2008) *Manga Shakespeare Macbeth*. London: Self Made Hero.

de Certeau, M. (1988) *The practice of everyday life*, trans. by S. Rendall. Berkeley and Los Angeles, CA: University of California Press.

Department for Education and Skills (DfES) (2002) *Framework for teaching English in secondary schools*. London: HMSO.

Dewey, J. (1920) *The child and the curriculum*. Chicago, IL: Chicago University Press.

Dewey, J. (2005) [1934] *Art as experience*. New York: Perigee Books.

Dixon, J. (1967) *Growth through English: A report based on the Dartmouth Seminar 1966*. Oxford: Oxford University Press.

Dixon, J. (1975) *Growth through English: Set in the perspective of the seventies*. Huddersfield: NATE.

Dixon, J. (1991) *A schooling in English: Critical episodes in the struggle to shape literary and cultural studies*. Buckingham: Open University Press.

Donaldson, J. and Scheffler, A. (1999) *The Gruffalo*. London: Macmillan Children's Books.

Eagleton, T. (1983) *Literary theory: An introduction*. Oxford: Blackwell.

Eagleton, T. (2000) *The idea of culture*. Oxford: Blackwell.

Egan, K. (1992) *Imagination in teaching and learning, ages 8–15*. London: Routledge.

Ellis, V., Fox, C. and Street, B. (2007) *Rethinking English in schools*. London and New York: Continuum.

Evans, J. (ed.) (2009) *Beyond the page: Reading and responding to picturebooks*. London: Routledge.

Fish, S. (1990) *Is there a text in this class?* Cambridge, MA: Harvard University Press.

Fowler, R. (1988) 'Oral models in the press', in M. Maclure, T. Phillips and A. Wilkinson (eds), *Oracy matters*. Milton Keynes: Open University Press.

Freire, P. (1996) [1970] *Pedagogy of the oppressed*, trans. by M. Bergman Ramos. London: Penguin.

Gardner, H. (1983) *Frames of mind: The theory of multiple intelligences*. London: Fontana Press.

Gardner, H. (1993) *Creating minds: An anatomy of creativity seen through the lives of Freud, Einstein, Stravinsky, Eliot, Graham, and Gandhi*. New York: Basic Books.

Gee, J.P. (2007) *What video games have to teach us about learning and literacy*. New York: Palgrave Macmillan.

Gibson, R. (1990) *Teaching Shakespeare*. Cambridge: Cambridge University Press.

Gilroy, P. (2002) *There ain't no black in the Union Jack: The cultural politics of race and nation*. London and New York: Routledge.

Giroux, H.A. (1987) 'Introduction: Literacy and the pedagogy of political empowerment', in P. Freire and D. Macedo, *Literacy: Reading the word and the world*. London: Routledge & Kegan Paul.

Goodwyn, A. (2004) *English teaching and the moving image*. London and New York: Routledge.

Grainger, T., Gooch, K. and Lambirth, A. (2005) *Creativity and writing: Developing voice and verve in the classroom*. London and New York: Routledge.

Grillo, O. (2009) *The Tempest: The complete play illustrated*. London: Can of Worms Publishing.

Haddon, M. (2005) *The curious incident of the dog in the night-time*. London: Vintage.

Harris, A., Jarvis, C. and Fisher, R. (2008) *Education in popular culture: Telling tales on teachers and learners*. London and New York: Routledge.

Hodder, I. (1998) 'Creative thought: A long-term perspective', in S. Mithen (ed.), *Creativity in human evolution and prehistory*. London and New York: Routledge, pp. 61–77.

Holbrook, D. (1961) *English for maturity: English in the secondary school*. Cambridge: Cambridge University Press.

Holbrook, D. (1964) *English for the rejected: Training literacy in the lower streams of the secondary school*. Cambridge: Cambridge University Press.

Holbrook, D. (1968) 'Creativity in the English Programme', in G. Summerfield (ed.), *Creativity in English: Papers relating to the Anglo-American Seminar on the Teaching of English at Dartmouth College, New Hampshire 1966*. Champaign, IL: NCTE.

Holmes, E. (1911) *What is and what might be: A study of education in general and elementary education in particular*. London: Richard Clay & Sons.

Hourd, M.L. (1949) *The education of the poetic spirit: A study in children's expression in the English lesson*. London: William Heinemann Ltd.

Hunter, I. (1988) *Culture and government: The emergence of literary education*. London: Macmillan.

Hutcheon, L. (2006) *A theory of adaptation*. London and New York: Routledge.

Iser, W. (1978) *The act of reading: A theory of aesthetic response*. London: Routledge & Kegan Paul.

Jeffrey, B. and Craft, A. (2003) 'Teaching creatively and teaching for creativity: distinctions and relationships', *Educational Studies*, 30(1), 77–87.

Kearney, R. (1988) *The wake of imagination: Ideas of creativity in Western culture*. London: Hutchinson Education.

Kearney, R. (2002) *On stories*. London and New York: Routledge.

Kelly, A.V. (2009) *The curriculum: Theory and practice*, 6th ed. London: Sage.

Khoury, E. (2006) *Gate of the sun*, trans. by H. Davies. London: Vintage.

Knights, B. and Thurgar-Dawson, C. (2006) *Active reading: Transformative writing in literary studies*. London and New York: Continuum.

Kress, G. (1982) *Learning to write*. London: Routledge & Kegan Paul.

Kress, G. (1993) 'Genre as social process', in B. Cope and M. Kalantzis, *The powers of literacy: A genre approach to teaching writing*. Pittsburgh, PA: University of Pittsburgh Press, pp. 22–37.

Kress, G. (1995) *Writing the future: English and the making of a culture of innovation*. Sheffield: NATE.

Kress, G. (2000) 'Multimodality', in B. Cope and M. Kalantzis (eds), *Multiliteracies: Literacy learning and the design of social futures*. London and New York: Routledge, pp. 182–202.

Kress, G. (2003) *Literacy in the New Media Age*. London and New York: Routledge.

Kress, G. (2010) *Multimodality: A social semiotic approach to contemporary communication*. London: Routledge.

Kress, G. and Van Leeuwen, T. (1995) *Reading images: The grammar of visual design*. London: Routledge.

Kress, G., Jewitt, C., Bourne, J., Franks, A., Hardcastle, J., Jones, K. and Reid, E. (2005) *English in urban classrooms: A multimodal perspective on teaching and learning*. London and New York: RoutledgeFalmer.

Laird, E. (2003) *A little piece of ground*. London: Macmillan Children's Books.

Lankshear, C. (1997) *Changing literacies*. Buckingham and Philadelphia, PA: Open University Press.

Leadbetter, C. (2000) *Living on thin air: The new economy with a blueprint for the 21st century*. London: Penguin.

Leavis, F.R. and Thompson, D. (1950) [1933] *Culture and environment: The training of critical awareness*. London: Chatto & Windus.

Lewis, D. (2001) *Reading contemporary picturebooks: Picturing text*. London and New York: Routledge.

Macmillan, M. (1904) *Education through the imagination*. London: Swan Sonnenschein & Co.

Madden, M. (2006) *99 ways to tell a story: Exercises in style*. London: Jonathan Cape.

Martin, J.R. (1989) *Factual writing: Exploring and challenging social reality*. Oxford: Oxford University Press.

Mathews, H. and Brotchie, A. (2005) *Oulipo compendium*. London: Atlas Press.

McCloud, S. (1994) *Understanding comics: The invisible art*. New York: HarperPerennial.

Mellor, B., Hemming, J. and Leggett, J. (1984) *Changing stories*. London: English and Media Centre.

Mercer, N. (1995) *The guided construction of knowledge: Talk amongst teachers and learners*. Clevedon: Multilingual Matters.

Mercer, N. and Hodgkinson, S. (2007) *Exploring talk in schools: Inspired by the work of Douglas Barnes*. Los Angeles, CA: Sage.

Misson, R. and Morgan, W. (2006) *Critical literacy and the aesthetic: Transforming the English classroom*. Urbana, IL: NCTE.

Misson, R. and Morgan, W. (2007) 'How critical is the aesthetic? The role of literature in English', in V. Ellis, C. Fox and B. Street, *Rethinking English in schools*. London and New York: Continuum, pp. 73–87.

Mitchell, D. (2004) *Cloud Atlas*. London: Sceptre.

Mithen, S. (1996) *The prehistory of the mind: A search for the origins of art, religion and science*. London: Phoenix.

Morgan, W. (1996) *Critical literacy in the classroom: The art of the possible*. London and New York: Routledge.

Myers, C. (2007) *Jabberwocky*. New York: Hyperion.

National Advisory Committee on Creative and Cultural Education (NACCCE) (1999) *All our futures*. London: DfEE.

New London Group (1996) 'A pedagogy of multiliteracies: Designing social futures', *Harvard Education Review*, 66, 60–92.

Nikolajeva, M. and Scott, C. (2006) *How picturebooks work*. London: Routledge.

Nodelman, P. (1990) *Words about pictures: The narrative art of children's picture books*. Athens, GA: University of Georgia Press.

Office for Standards in Education (Ofsted) (2010) *Learning: Creative approaches that raise standards*. London: HMSO.

Page, R. (ed.) (2010) *New perspectives on narrative and multimodality*. New York and London: Routledge.

Peim, N. (1993) *Critical theory and the English teacher: Transforming the subject*. London: Routledge.

Perec, G. (1994) *A void*, trans. by G. Adair. London: Harper Collins.

Petrus, H. and Butler, N. (2010) *Pride and prejudice*. New York: Marvel Classics.

Pope, R. (2005) *Creativity: Theory, history, practice*. London and New York: Routledge.

Powell, P. (2010) *The interrogative mood*. London: Profile Books.

QCA (2005) *Creativity: Find it; promote it!* London: HMSO.

QCDA (2007) *National Curriculum programme of study for English*. London: HMSO.

Queneau, R. (2009) *Exercises in style*, trans. by B. Wright. London: Oneworld Classics.

Ramachandran, V.S. (2011) *The tell-tale brain: Unlocking the mystery of human nature*. London: Heinemann.

Read, H. (1943) *Education through art*. London: Faber & Faber.

Reynolds, K. (2007) *Radical children's literature: Future visions and aesthetic transformations in juvenile fiction*. Basingstoke and New York: Macmillan Palgrave.

Rhodes, D. (2010) *Anthropology*. Edinburgh: Canongate.

Roberts, P. (2006) *Nurturing creativity in young people: A report to Government to inform future policy*. London: DfES.

Robinson, M. and Ellis, V. (2000) 'Writing in English and responding to writing', in J. Sefton-Green and R. Sinker (eds), *Evaluating creativity: Making and learning by young people*. London and New York: Routledge, pp. 70–88.

Rose, Jacqueline (1993) *The case of Peter Pan, or the impossibility of children's fiction*. Philadelphia, PA: University of Philadelphia Press.

Rose, Jonathan (2002) *The intellectual life of the British working classes*. New Haven, CT and London: Yale Nota Bene Press.

Rosen, H. (1985) *Stories and meanings*. Sheffield: NATE.

Rosen, H. (1988) 'The irrepressible gene', in M. Maclure, T. Phillips and A. Wilkinson (eds), *Oracy matters*. Milton Keynes: Open University Press.

Rosen, H. (1992) 'The politics of writing', in K. Kimberley, M. Meek and J. Miller (eds), *New readings: Contributions to an understanding of literacy*. London: A & C Black.

Rosenblatt, L. (1978) *The reader, the text, the poem: The transactional theory of the literary work*. Carbondale, IL: Southern Illinois University Press.

Ryman, G. (1998) *253*. London: HarperCollins.

Sachar, L. (2000) *Holes*. London: Bloomsbury.

Safford, K. and Barrs, M. (2005) *Creativity and literacy: Many routes to meaning*. London: Centre for Literacy in Primary Education.

Sampson, G. (1922) *English for the English: A chapter on national education*. Cambridge: Cambridge University Press.

Scholes, R. (1985) *Textual power: Literary theory and the teaching of English*. New Haven, CT and London: Yale University Press.

Scruton, R. (2000) 'After Modernism', *City Journal*, 10(2).

Sharples, M. (1999) *How we write: Writing as creative design*. London and New York: Routledge.

Shayer, D. (1972) *The teaching of English in schools 1900–1970*. London and Boston: Routledge & Kegan Paul.

Simpson, J. (1997) *Touching the void*. London: Vintage.

Sperber, D. (1996) *Explaining culture: A naturalistic approach*. Oxford: Blackwell Publishers.

Starko, A. (2010) *Creativity in the classroom: Schools of curious delight*. London and New York: Routledge.

Sutcliffe, W. (2004) *Bad influence*. London: Hamish Hamilton.

Swindells, R. (1993) *Stone cold*. London: Hamish Hamilton.

Szendy, P. (2008) *Listen: A history of our ears*. New York: Fordham University Press.

Tan, S. (2007) *The arrival*. London: Hodder.

Tan, S. (2010) *The lost thing*. London: Hodder.

Tomasello, M. (1999) *The cultural origins of human cognition*. Cambridge, MA: Harvard University Press.

Toop, D. (2010) *Sinister resonance: The mediumship of the listener*. New York: Continuum.

Tower, W. (2009) *Everything ravaged, everything burned*. London: Granta.

Tudor Owen, D. (1920) *The child vision: Being a study in mental development and expression*. Manchester: Manchester University Press.

Versaci, R. (2007) *This book contains graphic language: Comics as literature*. New York and London: Continuum.

Viola, W. (1942) *Child art*. London: University of London Press.

Volosinov, V.N. (2000) *Marxism and the philosophy of language*. Harvard, MA: Harvard University Press.

Vygotsky, L (1986) [1936] *Thought and language*. Cambridge, MA and London: The MIT Press.

Wells, C. (1986) *Children learning language and using language to learn*. London: Hodder & Stoughton.

Wilkinson, A. (1965) *Some aspects of oracy*. Sheffield: NATE.

Williams, R. (1958a) *Culture and society*. London: Hogarth Press.

Williams, R. (1958b) 'Culture is ordinary', in John Higgins (ed.) (2001), *The Raymond Williams reader*. Oxford: Blackwell Publishers.

Williams, R. (1961) *The long revolution*. London: Hogarth Press.

Williams, R. (1977) *Marxism and literature*. Oxford and New York: Oxford University Press.

Williams, R. (1983) *Keywords: A vocabulary of culture and society*. London: Routledge.

Willis, P. (1990) *Common culture: Symbolic work at play in the everyday cultures of the young*. Milton Keynes: Open University Press.

Winnicott, D.W. (1971) *Playing and reality*. London: Routledge.

Wolf, M. (2008) *Proust and the squid: The story and science of the reading brain*. Cambridge: Icon Books.

Zipes, J. (2006) *Why fairy tales stick: The evolution and relevance of a genre*. New York: Routledge.

Index

aesthetic, the 27, 28, 29–30, 76, 78
Alexander, Joy 90
Andrews, Richard 18, 54
Armstrong, Isabel 29–30
Arnold, Matthew 11
assessment 147
Attridge, Derek 2, 3, 30, 56, 57, 78, 80, 82, 133

Bakhtin, Mikhail 2, 28; speech genres 25, 103; listening 94
Browne, Anthony: *Hansel and Gretel* 48–9; *Me and You* 65
Browne, Eileen: *Handa's Surprise* 46–8
Bruner, Jerome 56

Carter, Ronald 2; spoken-written continuum 102–3, 105
Child, Lauren: *Goldilocks and the Three Bears* 65
'cognitive fluidity' *see* Steven Mithen
creativity: constraints to 5, 26, 115–16; definitions of 1, 9, 14, 20; and dialogue 14, 23, 25, 32, 54, 103, 112; of images 41; of language 20, 105; and literature 28; and modality 3; as pedagogical approach 12; relationship to culture 129–30; relationship to English 1, 2, 9, 20–1; symbolic 31; as transformative process 30, 32; of whole texts 47, 118; *see also* novels
critical-creativity 3, 111–28
critical literacy 15, 77, 113–14
cultural diversity 133, 144
culture 129–45; definitions of 129; memetic transmission of 134

Damassio, Antonio: human consciousness 40
'death of the author' 27
De Certeau, Michel: *The Practice of Everyday Life* 55, 61, 102

deconstruction 14, 15, 27
Dewey, John 29, 96
Dixon, John 15; *Growth through English* 13–14
Donaldson, Julia and Scheffler, Axel: *The Gruffalo* 49

Eagleton, Terry 14, 18
electronic communication 103–4
English teaching: 'creativity movement' 9, 12; Dartmouth seminar 13; design approach 112, 113; genre-based approach 16, 55; healthy English 33; history of subject 9, 14, 15; newspaper work 118–21; profile components 3; re-construction of 15; resources 56
evolution: of early humans 21; cultural 23
evolutionary shift 21
extreme re-creativity 55, 67–72; lipograms 71; multiple writings 68; noun + 7 70; possible worlds 73; prisoner's restriction 71

Fish, Stanley 76
Freire, Paulo 3, 111–12; banking concept of education 26, 114; dialogic language 25–6; *Pedagogy of the Oppressed* 26, 114; *praxis* 3, 115; problem-posing concept of education 26, 114; 'the word' 26, 114

Gee, James Paul *139, 141*
genre 16, 25, 66, 67; *see also* Kress, Gunther
Gibson, Rex 130
graphic novels 41, 45, 134–9
Grillo, Oscar: *The Tempest* 135

Holbrook, David 13; *English for Maturity* 12; *English for the Rejected* 12
hot-seating 92
Hourd, Margaret: *The Education of the Poetic Spirit* 12

Hunter, Ian 14
hypertext 143

idioculture 133
images *see* reading
imagination 27
intertextuality 44
Iser, Wolfgang 76

Kearney, Richard 2, 10; poetics of the possible 27; stories 28; postmodernism 56
Knights, Ben and Thurgar-Dawson, Chris 54
Kress, Gunther 2, 4; critique of critique 102; genre 16–17; language 102; multimodality 39; *not learning 146;* reading 39–40; synaesthesia 39; *Writing the Future* 17

Laird, Elizabeth: *A Little Piece of Ground* 96–101
language: change 44; creative capacity of 4; functions of 102; and learning 24; *see also* Kress, Gunther
learning: constraints to 5, 56;constructivist theory of 56; context of 133; in English 1; and language 24, 40–1; *not learning* 146–50; process of 31, 32; reflective 40; situated 32, 34; through talk 4, 13–14; *see also* language
Leavis, F.R. 11–12
listening 88–101; active 94–5; critical 95–101; dialogic 89, 95; 'with the ear' 90–4; *see also* Bakhtin, Mikhail
literary criticism 111, 128
literature 15, 62, 74; children's 83–4; as event 82; generative potential of 28; as stimuli for learning 62; role of story in 28

Manga Shakespeare 135–9
media 37
memetics 57
Misson, Ray and Morgan, Wendy 3, 16, 78
Mithen, Steven: 'cognitive fluidity' 21–2, 41, 73; *Prehistory of the Mind* 21
modality: definition of 37;of showing 75; of sound 50–1; of telling 75; verbal 38; visual 52, 135
modelling 93
Morgan, Wendy 113
multiculturalism 3, 132, 133
multimodality 17, 38; *see also* Kress, Gunther
Myers, Christopher: *Jabberwocky* 49

National Curriculum 10, 77
National Literacy Strategy 67

novels: *authoredness* in 78; creativity of 75, 77; ethics in 80; experience of 75, 76, 84, 87; importance of 75; *otherness* in 80; *textualness* in 78

ordinary creativity 4, 5, 30–1, 33
originality 57
Oulipo 68

picturebooks 41, 46–50
poetry 91–3
Pope, Rob 2, 56
post-structuralism 27
praxis see Freire, Paulo
Pride and Prejudice 139

Queneau, Raymond 4, 5, 68; *Exercises in Style* 68–9

'ratchet effect' *see* Tomasello, Michael
reader-response 27, 57, 62, 75
reading 52–3; active 3, 62–3; ages 74–5; choice 84–5; class readers 3; images 41–4; on screen 142–3; *see also* Kress Gunther
re-creativity: definition of 54, 56; learning function of 63–4; and new media technologies 55; and possible worlds 63; and reading 63; and re-telling 55, 58–61; and re-writing 55, 62; stimulation for 56; and transforming novels 65; and *writer-response* 55, 57, 62–3
re-drafting 124–7; *see also* Vygotsky, Lev
role-play 122–3, 141
Romantic poets 9, 11, 27
Rosen, Harold 55, 58, 62
Rosenblatt, Louise 76

Sampson, George 10–11; 13; *English for the English* 10, 90
schools: popular representations of 9
self-expression 11, 14
Shakespeare, William 134–9
sound tunnels 92
speaking and writing 102–9; differences between 105
spoken-written continuum *see* Ronald Carter
standards 146
story-telling 27, 28
structuralism 27
students as teachers 122–3, 141
synaesthesia 38–9, 73; *see also* Kress, Gunther

Tan, Sean: *The Arrival* 42, 43, 44, 45; *The Lost Thing* 50–1

Tomasello, Michael: 'ratchet effect' 22; symbolic language 22
transaction, processes of 3, 27, 75, 76
transduction 45, 55

video games 139–42
voice 58, 62, 94, 98
Volosinov, Valentin 2, 24–5
Vygotsky, Lev 2, 105; and inner speech 23–4; on language and thought 23, 40, 52; on

re-drafting 107, 123; and 'shower of words' 41, 45, 77, 91; on writing 118, 123

Williams, Raymond 130–2, 145
Willis, Paul 131
Winnicott, D.W. 30–1, 122, 123
Wolf, Maryanne 52–3
Writing 63, 109, 123–4; constraints in 67–8; as process 14; using text types 67; *see also* Vygotsky, Lev